Webster's New World™
Dictionary of
Eponyms

Common Words from Proper Names

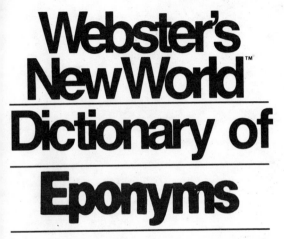

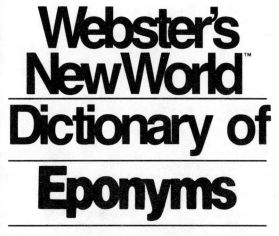

Webster's New World™

Dictionary of

Eponyms

Common Words from Proper Names

Auriel Douglas

Webster's New World

New York London Toronto Sydney Tokyo Singapore

Much of this book is based on *Webster's New World Dictionary, Third College Edition* © 1988 by Simon & Schuster, Inc.

 **WEBSTER'S
NEW WORLD**

Simon & Schuster, Inc.
15 Columbus Circle
New York, NY 10023

DISTRIBUTED BY PRENTICE HALL TRADE SALES

Manufactured in the United States of America

1 2 3 4 5 6 7 8 9 10

Library of Congress Cataloging-in-Publication Data

Douglas, Auriel.
    Webster's New World dictionary of eponyms : common words from proper names / Auriel Douglas.
        p.   cm.
    ISBN 0-13-949926-1
    1. English language—Eponyms—Dictionaries. 2. Names, Personal—Dictionaries. 3. Biography—Dictionaries. I. Title. II. Title: Dictionary of eponyms.
PE1596.D68   1990
423'.1—dc20   90-12181
                                                          CIP

DEDICATED TO:

Librarians everywhere, and especially to
Marilyn Saunders, Agnes Song, Elena
Panajotovic, and Meri Martha Wascsepinecz
of the Beverly Hills, California Public
Library. Also, with thanks to PC Professor
Robert Neal Marshall.

EPONYM – noun. 1. A real or mythical person whose name is or is thought to be the source of the name of a city, country, era, institution, or the like: "Romulus" is the eponym of Rome. 2. A real or fictitious person whose name has become synonymous with an era, event, object, practice, or the like.

Preface

The ultimate tribute to anyone is to have his or her name incorporated into the language. What makes eponyms—common words from uncommon people—so much fun is that behind every word is a fascinating story. These words reflect the entire range of human endeavor and human nature. Some people got their names into the dictionary by being stubborn (see MAVERICK), some by being dignified (see GREAT SCOTT!), and some by being foolish (see BRODIE). But each one did something outstanding, or exhibited a human trait in such a pronounced manner, that it has forever after been associated with that person.

Every effort has been made to include the dates of each person's birth and death so that the reader can place them in the proper historical perspective. Where no dates are given, none were available.

I have excluded the names of cities, airports, boulevards, and places for the most part because their origins are obvious: Washington, D.C., Kennedy Airport, etc. The names of stars, planets, comets (except for Halley's!) are also left out for the same reason. For the most part *places* are named for kings, queens, presidents, and the like. With one exception, the story behind the naming of the city of CLEVELAND amused me and so I included it. I hope it also amuses you.

AURIEL DOUGLAS

A

AARON'S ROD Any of several flowering plants having tall, erect stems. In architecture, a rod-shaped molding decorated with a design of leaves, scrolls, or a twined serpent.

Aaron The original high priest of the Hebrew nation, the older brother of Moses (Exodus 28:1–4; 40:12–23). Both are named after the rod of Aaron which blossomed and produced almonds (Numbers 17:8).

ABIGAIL A lady's maid.

Abigail The name of a serving maid in *The Scornful Lady* (1614), a play by Beaumont and Fletcher.

ACHAEMENID A member of the ruling dynasty of Persia from the time of Cyrus the Great to the death of Darius III (533–300 B.C.).

Akhaimenes Persian king, the eponymous founder of the dynasty.

ACHATES A loyal friend.

Achates In the *Aeneid*, the faithful companion of Aeneas.

ACHILLES HEEL A vulnerable or susceptible spot.

Achilles In Greek myth, a warrior and leader in the Trojan War who killed Hector and was in turn killed by Paris with an arrow that struck his only vulnerable spot, his heel. He is the hero of Homer's *Iliad*. Also *Achilles tendon*, the tendon connecting the back of the heel to the muscles of the calf of the leg.

ADAM Neoclassic style of furniture and architecture.

Robert Adam (1728–1792) Scottish architect, the most important of four brothers, the others being John, James, and William. Robert was the architect to King George III. With James and William, he built a section of London called the Adelphia section. With James, he built many public buildings and private mansions. The Adam brothers introduced a light, decorative style of furniture characterized by wreaths, patterns such as the honeysuckle and the fan ornament.

ADAMSITE A yellow crystalline compound dispersed in air as a poisonous gas.

Rogers Adam (b. 1889) American chemist who developed the compound.

ADDISON'S DISEASE A usually fatal disease caused by the failure of the adrenal cortex to function.

Thomas Addison (1793–1860) English physician who discovered this disease in 1855 when he was a resident at Guy's Hospital in London.

ADDISONIAN TERMINATION Ending a sentence with a preposition such as "to," "of" or "with."

Joseph Addison (1672–1719) English essayist, dramatist, statesman, and poet, best known by his contemporaries for his tragedy *Cato*, produced at Drury Lane in 1713. He annoyed critic Richard Hurd by ending many of his sentences with a preposition.

ADLERIAN PSYCHOLOGY A school of psychology which believes that behavior arises in a subconscious effort to compensate for inferiority or deficiency and that neurosis results from overcompensation.

Alfred Adler (1870–1937) Viennese psychologist and psychiatrist who, at first a Freudian, later opposed Freud's emphasis on sex and advanced his own theory of the inferiority complex to explain psychopathic cases. (See FREUDIAN.)

ADONIC A measure used in verses.

Adonis In Greek mythology, a youth known for his beauty. The Adonic meter was said to be first used in verses lamenting Adonis' death.

ADONIS A young man of striking beauty.

Adonis In Greek mythology, a young man of great beauty, loved by Aphrodite because of his good looks. He loved hunting and was killed during the chase by a wild boar.

AEGIS also EGIS Protection, sponsorship, patronage.

Aegis In Greek mythology, the shield of Zeus lent by him to Athena. There would be no greater protection than being guarded by Zeus' shield.

AEOLIAN HARP A musical instrument, also called the "wind harp."

Aeolus In Greek mythology, the god of the wind.

AESCULAPIAN Of or pertaining to the healing arts, medical.

Aesculapius The Roman god of medicine and healing.

ALEXANDER'S BEARD Clean shaven.

Alexander the Great (*356–323 B.C.*) He was always shown beardless.

ALEXANDERS Any of several plants of the genus *Zizia* or related genera, especially Golden Alexanders.

Alexander the Great (356–323 b.c.) The inspiration for this plant's name since its brilliant color suggested royalty.

ALICE BLUE Pale blue.

Alice Roosevelt Longworth (1884–1980) Daughter of Theodore Roosevelt; Alice wore the color frequently, so much so that it came to be called "Alice Blue." She and her favorite color are immortalized in the song "My Beautiful Alice Blue Gown." A fiery, independent personality, Alice once said, "I hate gossip. But if you have any, sit beside me." When Theodore Roosevelt was asked why he didn't control his daughter, he stated: "I can either run this country or control Miss Alice. I cannot do both." When Alice married Nicholas Longworth, who was speaker of the house from 1925 to 1931, everyone expected her to settle down. She didn't.

ALZHEIMER'S DISEASE A progressive, irreversible disease characterized by degeneration of the brain cells and leading to severe dementia.

A. Alzheimer (1864–1915) German physician who first described it.

AMATI A highly-prized violin made by a member of the Amati family.

Nicolò Amati (1596–1684) Master Italian violin-maker of Cremona, teacher of Stradivari and Guarneri. (See STRADIVARIUS and GUARNERIUS.)

AMAZON A large, strong, masculine woman.

Amazon In Greek mythology, any of a race of female warriors believed to have lived in Scythia, near the Black Sea. The word actually means "without breast," since the Amazons were said to have cut off one breast to facilitate their use of the bow and arrow.

AMAZON ANT Any of several small red ants of the genus *Polyergus* that take over and enslave the young of other species.

Amazons These female warriors (see AMAZON) were said to raise captured children, which is why the ant is so named.

AMBROSIAN CHANT A type of chant introduced by St. Ambrose, still used today in the Cathedral in Milan.

St. Ambrose (A.D. 340?–397) Bishop of Milan. His feast day is December 7. The chant which bears his name is characterized by a greater ornamentation of melody than in the Gregorian chant, which superseded it. (See GREGORIAN.)

AMERICA   The United States of America, South America, Central America.

Americus Vespuccius (1451–1512)   Latin form of the name for Amerigo Vespucci, Italian navigator for whom America was named. He explored the New World coastline after Columbus. His accounts of his journeys were published in 1507 by Martin Waldseemüller, a German geographer, who suggested the new lands be named "America" and added that name to the maps he had drawn from Amerigo's descriptions.

AMISH   A sect of Mennonites, or Plain People, that settled in the United States.

Jacob Ammann   A Swiss Mennonite bishop who led a group away from that church in Switzerland. His followers became known as Amish or Amish Mennonites. The Ammann schism took place from 1693–1697.

AMPERE   The standard unit for measuring the strength of an electric current.

André Marie Ampère (1775–1836)   A French scientist, professor of physics at the College de France, Paris in 1824. He discovered important principles in the field of magnetism and electricity, formulated Ampere's law which forms the basis of the study of electrodynamics, and invented the astatic needle.

The ampere, or unit of intensity of an electric current, is quite rightly named after him.

ANACREONTIC In the manner of the poems of Anacreon, specifically convivial or amatory.

Anacreon (572?–488? B.C.) A Greek poet noted for his songs praising love and wine.

ANNIE OAKLEY A free ticket or pass.

Annie Oakley (1860–1926) A famous American markswoman who starred in Buffalo Bill's Wild West Show (1885–1902). Her real name was Phoebe Anne Oakley Mozee. A free ticket or pass is called an "Annie Oakley" because her small targets resembled punched tickets.

APHRODISIAC Arousing or increasing sexual desire.

Aphrodite In Greek mythology, the goddess of love and beauty.

APOLLO Any young man of great physical beauty.

Apollo In Greek and Roman mythology, the god of music, poetry, prophecy, and medicine, represented as exemplifying manly youth and beauty.

APPIAN WAY An ancient paved road in Italy, extending about 350 miles between Rome and Brindisi.

Appius Claudius Caecus (circa 300 B.C.) A Roman censor from 312–307 B.C., consul (307 B.C.) and dictator. He ordered the Appian Way to be built in 312 B.C. and promptly put his name on the first signpost. Appius was famed for many reforms. He gave more privileges to the ordinary people than they'd known before, and is credited with founding Latin prose and oratory.

APPLESEED, JOHNNY A famous pseudonym for John Chapman.

John Chapman (1774–1845) Legendary American who gained his nickname between 1800 and 1810 when he ranged widely over the country planting apple seeds and pruning the growing trees. He's the subject of many legends and is celebrated in literature in Vachel Lindsay's *In Praise of Johnny Appleseed.*

ARACHNID Any of various arthropods of the class Arachnida, such as spiders, scorpions, mites, or ticks, characteristically having four pairs of legs.

Arachne In Greek mythology, a maiden who was transformed into a spider by Athena for challenging the goddess to a weaving contest, and then insulting the gods.

ARGOSY A large merchant ship; a fleet of such ships.

Argo In Greek mythology, the ship in which Jason sailed in search of the Golden Fleece.

ARGUS Any alert, watchful person.
ARGUS-EYED Extremely observant, vigilant.

Argus In Greek mythology, a giant with a hundred eyes who was made guardian of Io and later slain by Hermes.

ARGYLE Knitted or woven in a pattern of diamond-shaped figures of different colors.

3rd Duke of Argyll, Archibald Campbell (1682–1761) Lord high treasurer of Scotland in 1705, Scottish representative peer in 1707, and justice general in 1710. He was Walpole's chief adviser in Scotland and keeper of the Great Seal from 1734–1761. Argyll was the Scottish title of the peerage of the Campbell family, and the duke is chiefly remembered because he had the Argyll clan tartan knitted or woven into his socks.

ARIANISM In theology, the doctrine that denies that Jesus was of the same substance as God and states that he was only the highest of created beings.

Arius (d. A.D. 336) An Alexandrian theologian, born in Libya, and not surprisingly condemned as a heretic at the Council of Nicaea (325).

ARRAS   A wall hanging, especially of tapestry.

Arras   A city in northern France noted for its 15th-century tapestries.

ARTHURIAN   Of or pertaining to King Arthur and his knights of the Round Table.

King Arthur   Legendary British hero said to have been king of England in the 6th century A.D.

ATHENEUM   An institution, such as a literary club or scientific academy, a library, and a Roman school of art founded by the Roman emperor Hadrian (A.D. 76–138).

Athena   The Greek goddess of wisdom and the arts. In the temple of Athena at Athens philosophy and art were taught.

ATLANTIC   The Atlantic Ocean. The second largest on earth, extending from the Arctic in the north to the Antarctic in the south, and from the Americas in the west to Europe and Africa in the east.

Atlas   Figure in Greek mythology. Atlas's name is represented in *Atlantis*, a legendary island in the Atlantic west of Gibraltar, said by Plato to have sunk beneath the sea.

ATLAS   Any person who carries a great burden or is extraordinarily powerful; a book of maps.

Atlas   In Greek mythology, a Titan compelled to support the heavens on his shoulders. Atlas supporting the earth was often pictured on the front page of books of maps, tables, charts, illustrations, etc., on a specific subject or subjects such as an anatomical atlas. Atlas has also lent his name to an intercontinental ballistic missile of the U.S. Air Force.

ATROPHY   To waste away, to wither.

Atropos   In Greek mythology, one of the three Fates; she is represented as cutting the thread of life.

ATTICISM   An expression characterized by conciseness and elegance.

Attic   The ancient Greek dialect of Athens in which the bulk of classical Greek literature is written.

AUGEAN   Exceedingly filthy from long neglect.

Augeas   In Greek mythology, legendary king of Elis, who left his stables uncleaned for thirty years.

AUGUST   The eighth month of the year.

Augustus Caesar (63 B.C.–A.D. 14)   Adopted son of Julius Caesar, whose real name was Gaius Octavius; he was known as Octavian. He was the founder of the imperial Roman government. He received the exalted title of "Augustus" (sacred) conferred by the Senate in 27 B.C.

AVALON The main town of Catalina Island, one of the Santa Barbara Islands, a resort center 75 square miles at sea lying 24 miles southwest of Los Angeles, California.

Avalon In Celtic myth, an island paradise in the western seas where King Arthur and other heroes went after death.

B

BABBITT A philistine, a person indifferent to everything but business success.

George Babbitt Name of a character in Sinclair Lewis's novel (1922), a smugly conventional person interested chiefly in business and social success and indifferent to cultural values.

BABBLE To utter a meaningless confusion of words or sounds.

Babel A city (now thought to be Babylon) in Shinar where, according to the Book of Genesis, the construction of a heaven-reaching tower was interrupted by the confusion of tongues.

BABYLONIAN Characterized by a luxurious, pleasure-seeking, and immoral way of life.

13

Babylonia An ancient empire in the lower Euphrates Valley of southwestern Asia, prominent from about 2000 to 1000 B.C. The capital, Babylon, was a place of great luxury and corruption.

BACCHANAL A dance or song in honor of Bacchus. Also, *Bacchanalia*, an ancient Roman festival in honor of Bacchus; *bacchant*, a worshiper of Bacchus; *bacchante*, a priestess or woman admirer of Bacchus.

Bacchus An ancient Greek and Roman god of wine and revelry, earlier called Dionysus by the Greeks. (By the way, all the above definitions have their negative side. They are: *bacchanal*, a drunken carouser; *bacchanalia*, a drunken party, an orgy; *bacchant*, given to drunken carousing; and *bacchante*, an inebriated carousing woman.)

BACITRACIN An antibiotic isolated from a bacillus.

Margaret Tracy An American child, born 1936, in whose tissues it was first found.

BADMINTON A game played by volleying a shuttlecock back and forth over a net by means of a long-handled racket.

Badminton House A stately home, owned by the Duke of Beaufort, where the game was often played. This game was introduced into England about 100 years ago by army officers who had seen it played in

India, where it is called Poona. Malaysia, Thailand, and other parts of Southeast Asia, where the game has been played for many centuries, produce more good players than other countries. Malaysia won the first official world championship, beating Denmark.

BAEDEKER   A guidebook.

Karl Baedeker (1801–1859)   A printer and publisher in Germany who became famous by publishing an excellent series of guidebooks, a separate one for each country in Europe. "Have you got your Baedeker?" became a common inquiry among tourists 100 years ago. Travelers could thus learn all about such things as palaces, museums, libraries, art exhibits, castles, schools, and other famous landmarks. So popular were Karl's books that the term "baedeker" soon replaced "guidebook" as a generic term.

BAILEY BRIDGE   A steel bridge designed to be shipped in parts and assembled rapidly.

Sir Donald Coleman Bailey (b. 1901)   Inventor of the convertible bridge, which he developed when he was an engineer with the British Ministry of Supply. He was knighted in 1945 for this contribution. The Bailey Bridge is still pressed into use today, especially when the structures are destroyed by tornadoes, floods, etc.

BAKELITE   A trademark for any of a group of plastics having high chemical and electrical resistance.

Leo H. Baeckland (1863–1944) Chemist and inventor, born in Belgium and educated at the University of Ghent. Baeckland was a manufacturer of photographic papers of his own invention and is best known for his discovery of the synthetic resin bakelite.

BALBOA The basic monetary unit of Panama, equal to 100 centesimos.

Vasco Núñez de Balboa (1475–1519) Spanish explorer who sailed to America about 1500. He discovered the Pacific Ocean and took formal possession of it for Spain on September 29, 1513. He served under Pedrarias, the new governor of Panama, with whom he had many disputes. Balboa was accused (the history books say "probably falsely") of sedition and executed.

BALDWIN A red-skinned American variety of apple.

Colonel Loammi Baldwin (1740–1807) Revolutionary war soldier who settled down in Massachusetts, and later Virginia, and turned his attention to developing, perfecting, and growing the apple which bears his name.

BALONEY Bologna; also, foolish or exaggerated talk, nonsense.

Bologna, Italy Italian city which lies at the foot of the Apennine Mountains, about 185 miles northwest of Rome. It has been a center of culture for nearly two thousand years. The people of Bologna manufacture many things, including soap, silk, candles, and musical instruments. It is also known for its churches, which are beautiful and contain thousands of art treasures. A kind of sausage from Bologna has become famous as "baloney."

BARMECIDE FEAST Any pretended generosity.

Prince Barmecide The name of a character in *The Arabian Nights* who served a pretended feast with no food. Since then it has come to be known for any pretended or illusory generosity or hospitality.

BARTLETT PEAR A large juicy variety of pear.

Enoch Bartlett (1779–1860) Distributor who got all the credit for this popular fruit, known in France and England as the "bon chrétien." It was introduced to America by Captain Thomas Brewer and grown on his farm at Roxbury, Massachusetts. By all rights it should have been called the "Brewer pear" because Enoch Bartlett simply distributed it; however he distributed it under his own name after he bought Brewer's farm.

BAYONET A knife adapted to fit the muzzle end of a rifle and used in close combat.

Bayonne, France Seaport of southwestern France, 13 miles north of the Spanish border, where the bayonet was first made.

BEAU BRUMMELL A fashionable man, a dandy, a fop.

George Bryan Brummell (1778–1840) An Englishman known for his fastidious dress and manners. During his time men's clothes were changing greatly. The old style had been knee-breeches, very frilly shirts, and brightly colored coats. Beau Brummell favored styles that were not too fancy. Beau, who attended the best English schools, made friends with many important people including the Prince of Wales, who later became King George IV. He soon became a fashion advisor to the Prince. Later, he quarreled with the prince and went to France where he died in poverty in a charity hospital in 1840, at age 62.

BÉCHAMEL A rich sauce.

Louis de Béchamel (d. 1703) A French financier and gastronome, steward to Louis XIV. King Louis was so fond of Béchamel's sauce of cream, flour, and butter that he and the court allowed him to name it after himself.

BEDLAM Any place or situation of noisy uproar and confusion.

St. Mary of Bethlehem   Bedlam was an English corruption of Bethlehem (Hebrew: house of bread). Before the 17th century the word *bedlam* was also used for the city in Palestine. The hospital of St. Mary of Bethlehem in London, founded in 1247, since 1547 has been used as a state insane asylum, a madhouse. Hence *bedlam* connotes the confusion and noise one might expect from a group of insane people.

BEEF WELLINGTON   Beef, liver pâté, bacon, and brandy with seasonings all cooked in a golden crust of puff pastry.

Arthur Wellesley, 1st Duke of Wellington (1769–1852)   English nobleman known as the "Iron Duke." His chef, name unknown, concocted this rich dish for the Duke, and it was one of his favorites. (See WELLINGTON BOOT).

BEG   To ask for charity or a gift.

Lambert le Begue   A pious monk known as "the stammerer." An order of nuns, called *Beguines*, was established in his honor in Liège in the 12th century. Shortly afterwards, in the Netherlands, a male order was established. As many of them were mendicants the term took on its present meaning.

BEGONIA   A family of tropical plants grown for their handsome ornamental leaves or their clustered, showy flowers.

Michael Bégon (1638–1710)   A French Administrator, posted in the French West Indies, who admired the lavish, showy tropical foliage, so unlike the smaller, paler blooms of his native land. An avid patron of the sciences who made regular financial contributions to its cause, after his arduous tour of duty Michael brought back to France some examples of a flower he particularly liked. His enthusiasm for the flower or, perhaps, his generous financial contributions to scientific endeavors, caused it to be named after him.

BENDAY PROCESS   A method of adding a tone to a printed image by imposing a transparent sheet of dots or other patterns on the image at some stage of the photographic reproduction process.

Benjamin Day (1838–1916)   A New York printer who invented the method.

BENEDICT   A traitor; also a newlywed man who had seemed a confirmed bachelor.

Benedict Arnold (1741–1804)   An American general in the Revolutionary War. He is remembered as a brave and skillful soldier, but unfortunately also as a traitor, who betrayed his country and went over to the British side. The British, too, despised him as a traitor and he lived a very unhappy life there until he died in 1804. **Benedick** A character in Shakespeare's *Much Ado About Nothing*, marries Beatrice after a long bachelorhood.

BERSERK Destructively or frenetically violent; deranged.

The Scandinavian Hero Berserk A fictionalized character in Norse mythology, a fierce warrior who fought in battle with frenzied violence. He had twelve sons, *berserkers,* whose violence terrified the land. Hence, to go berserk.

BERTHA A wide, deep collar, often of lace, that covers the shoulders of a low-necked dress.

Queen Bertha of the Big Foot (d. 783) Mother of Charlemagne (King of the Franks, 768–814). The fashions of the day called for low-cut gowns but this modest woman had her dressmaker sew collars to cover her shoulders and bosom. They soon became known as "Berthas."

BIBB LETTUCE A lettuce formed in loose heads of very crisp, dark leaves.

Jack Bibb (1789–1884) An amateur gardener who developed the lettuce in his backyard in Frankfort, Kentucky, about 1850.

BIG BEN The great bell in the parliament clock tower in London; also refers to the clock itself.

Sir Benjamin Hall The Commissioner in charge when Big Ben was installed in 1856. The bell measures 9 feet across and weighs 13½ tons. When it was first cast a crack was discovered while it was being tested, and so it was melted again and recast. Londoners will argue that "Big Ben" is not the name of the clock, but of the bell which chimes the hour. Incidentally, the first stroke of Big Ben, and not the last, is the exact hour.

BIG BERTHA A large gun with a claimed range of 75 miles.

Bertha Krupp von Vohlen und Halbach (1886–1937) Granddaughter of the founder of the Krupp Munitions Works at Essen; control passed to her after the death of her father. It was under her management that the gun was created during World War I. Because of its long range, its announced intention was to bomb Paris from safely within the German lines. The name is actually a translation of the German *dicke bertha* or fat Bertha.

BIKINI A very brief two-piece bathing suit for women.

Bikini Atoll In the Marshall Islands, site of atomic bomb tests in 1946. The bathing suit got its name from the atoll because its effect on the viewer was said to resemble that of an atomic bomb.

BILLINGSGATE   Foul-mouthed abuse.

Billingsgate   A fish market in London notorious for the foul language and abusive talk used there by the fishmongers and fishwives.

BILLYCOCK HAT   A type of felt hat with a low, round crown, as a derby.

William "Billy" Coke   Well-known Londoner called "Billy" Coke; he introduced and popularized this type of hat at the shooting parties held at Holkham, around about the 1850s. Hatters of old established London West End shops still refer to these hats as "Coke hats."

BINET SCALE   A test for measuring intelligence.

Alfred Binet (1857–1911)   A French psychologist, born in Nice. He was director of the psychology laboratory at the Sorbonne in Paris. He collaborated with Theodore Simon in establishing a standard by which degrees of intelligence could be measured.

BISCUIT TORTONI   A rich ice-cream dessert usually flavored with almonds, often garnished with whipped cream, and served in a paper cup.

Tortoni   (first name unknown) A 19th-century French restaurateur in Paris who is usually given credit for whipping up the dessert one day.

BLACK MARIA   Colloquial term for a prison van.

Maria Lee   The owner of a sailor's lodging house in Boston; she was a large and powerful Afro-American. On one occasion, seeing a policeman overpowered she went to his aid and rescued him, at the same time apprehending the attacker. Afterwards she assisted the police on a number of occasions, so much so that recalling her strength the police, when an offender was troubling them, sent out an SOS, "Send for Black Maria."

BLANKET   A large piece of wool or other thick cloth used as a covering for warmth, especially on a bed.

Thomas Blanket (circa 1380)   An Englishman, who first made these coverings late in the 14th century.

BLARNEY   Smooth talk used in flattering or coaxing.

Blarney Castle   A castle near Cork, Ireland. In 1662 when besieged by the English, Cormach Macarthy asked for an armistice. Instead of surrendering at the time agreed upon, he sent out evasive excuses, until the English commander realized he'd been duped. The incident gave rise to the expression, "None of your Blarney." High up in the wall of Blarney Castle is a stone commemorating this event. The legend regarding the stone is that anybody who can reach and kiss it will be able to obtain anything he desires by talk.

BLIMP   A smug, unprogressive person.

Colonel Blimp   A character created between the World Wars by British cartoonist David Low; Blimp was a pompous, smug, highly conservative person.

BLOODY MARY   A drink made with vodka, tomato juice, and seasonings.

Mary Tudor (1516–1558)   Queen of England and Ireland from 1553 to 1558; she was nicknamed "Bloody Mary." The daughter of Henry VIII, she succeeded to the throne on the death of her half brother, Edward VI. She repealed the laws which had established Protestantism in England and re-established Roman Catholicism. She persecuted the Protestants, the total number killed during her reign being about 300. The connection between the color of the drink and all the blood Mary spilled is obvious.

BLOOMER   A short skirt and loose trousers gathered at the ankles.

Amelia Jenks Bloomer (1818–1894)   A United States feminist and social reformer and editor of the reformist *Lily* (1848–1854). She championed temperance and women's rights and the wearing of a costume which would free women from heavy, often multi-layered skirts. The costume, which she herself wore, consisted of a short skirt with loose trousers gathered at the ankles, called a "bloomer." It took Marlene Dietrich in the early 1930s to popularize the idea and by then they were called slacks.

BLUCHERS   Heavy half boots.

Field Marshal Gebhart Leberecht von Blücher (1742–1819)   A Prussian field marshal with a very active military service. He served in the campaign of 1805–1806 at Ratkow, near Lubeck; he was a general and commander in Pomerania in 1809–1811; and after the outbreak of the War of Liberation, led Prussian troops under Russian command at Lutzen, Bautzen, Haynau, etc. In 1813 he became commander in chief of the Silesian army (Prussians and Russians). He was awarded a special Iron Cross by Frederick William III. Of course he's best known for the type of very heavy half boots that he favored wearing on and off the battlefield.

BLUEBEARD   A murderer.

Bluebeard   A fictionalized character in Charles Perrault's story "Barbe Bleu," published in 1697. He married and then murdered one wife after another.

BOBBY   (British colloquial) A policeman.

Sir Robert Peel (1788–1850)   A politician who re-organized the London police force. Peel's peace-keeping philosophy was: never instigate, never create, never envision; direct all your energy toward maintaining the status quo and accept change only when it has become obvious to everyone that you cannot keep the peace any other way. Peel managed to institute many reforms in criminal law that had been advocated unsuccessfully for years, including the abolition of the death penalty for petty offenses. (It was retained only for murder, treason, and forging a Bank of England note.) Among the many political offices he held were: undersecretary for war and colonies, chief secretary for Ireland, house secretary, first lord of treasury, and prime minister (1841). The poet Byron, who was in the same class with him at Harrow, wrote of him, "As a scholar, he was greatly my superior; as a declaimer and actor, I was reckoned at least his equal; as a schoolboy out of school, I was always in scrapes—he never."

BODONI   A style of typeface.

Giambattista Bodoni (1740–1813)   Italian printer and type designer; he designed the first roman type style now called "modern." He published editions of Homer's *Iliad*, Virgil, and multilingual editions of the Lord's Prayer.

BOLÍVAR   The monetary unit of Venezuela.

Simón Bolívar (1783–1830)   South American soldier, statesman, and revolutionary leader known as El Libertador—the liberator. Among his many accomplishments, he freed Peru from Spain (acting as president from 1823–1827) and organized a new republic—named Bolivia after himself.

BOOLEAN ALGEBRA   Algebraic systems based on symbolic logic.

George Boole (1815–1864)   An English mathematician and logician, a professor at Queen's College, Cork, and author of many books on differential equations, calculus, mathematical theories of logic, and probabilities, in which he elaborated his method of applying mathematics to logic.

BOOZE   An alcoholic drink, liquor.

E. G. Booz (circa 1840)   A distiller in Philadelphia, he sold his "booze" under his own name, the whiskey packaged in bottles shaped like a log cabin. No doubt he popularized the term but the Oxford English Dictionary states it was in use in 1529.

BOSC   A sweet russet winter pear.

L. Bosc d'Antic (1759–1823)   French naturalist who developed the fruit.

BOSTON   A card game for four players using two decks of cards.

Boston   The capital city of Massachusetts. The terms used in the game refer to the siege of the city in 1775–1776, during the Revolutionary War, and the Battle of Bunker Hill which took place in 1775.

BOSWELL   An assiduous and devoted admirer, student, and recorder of another's words and deeds.

James Boswell (1740–1795)   Scottish lawyer and biographer of Samuel Johnson. Boswell met Dr. Johnson in London in 1763, visited him frequently, toured with him, took notes unceasingly of Dr. Johnson's conversations, and finally wrote his masterpiece of biography, *The Life of Samuel Johnson*, in 1791. If you want to flatter a biographer and give him the highest praise, call him a "Boswell."

BOUGAINVILLAEA   A genus of woody tropical vines of the four-o-clock family, having inconspicuous flowers surrounded by large, showy, purple or red bracts.

Louis Antoine de Bougainville (1729–1811)   A soldier who liked to stop and smell the flowers. This French navigator and aide-de-camp to Montcalm in Canada served in Germany in the Seven Years' War, and made an unsuccessful attempt to colonize the Falkland Islands for France. He commanded the first French expedition to sail around the world and visited Tuamotu, Tahiti, the Samoan group, part of the New Hebrides, and the Louisiade (sic) and New

Britain archipelagoes. He brought home a showy tropical flowering vine which, after all he'd been through on behalf of his country, was thoughtfully named for him.

BOURBON   A whiskey distilled from a fermented mash containing not less than 51 percent corn.

Bourbon County, Kentucky   Place where bourbon was originally made; the county in turn, was named after the French royal family.

BOWDLERIZE   To expurgate prudishly.

Thomas Bowdler (1754–1825)   English editor who was so offended by some of William Shakespeare's words that in 1818 he published a *Family Shakespeare*, which was an expurgated version omitting or modifying parts which he said "cannot with any propriety be read aloud in a family." His 10-volume bowdlerized Shakespeare was popular but his prudishness also amused readers and it soon gave rise to the opprobrious word *bowdlerize*.

BOWIE KNIFE   A steel knife about fifteen inches long, with a single edge, carried in a sheath, originally used by American frontiersmen as a weapon.

Col. James Bowie (1799–1836)   American frontiersman who shunned the hand weapons of the day and made his own. It was a handy device to have

30

when he settled in Texas about 1820, and when he became a naturalized Mexican citizen in 1830, even handier. James opposed the central Mexican government in 1832, and later became a colonel in the Texas army. He was killed at the Alamo on March 6, 1836. Although Col. James popularized the bowie knife, there are some who believe that his brother Rezin, also a frontiersman, may have actually designed it.

BOWLER   A derby hat.
   William Bowler   An English hatmaker circa 1861 who made this type of men's hat.

BOYCOTT   To join together in refusing to deal with, so as to punish, coerce, etc.; to refuse to buy, sell, or use.
   Captain C.C. Boycott (1832–1897)   A retired British army captain who became an agent for estates in County Mayo, Ireland, in 1873. During the Land League agitation of 1880, his Irish neighbors ostracized him socially and economically because of the position he held. Ever since, this unfortunate man's name has meant someone or something that one would unconditionally refuse to deal with.

BOYLE'S LAW   A chemical law which states that if the body of gas is at constant temperature, then the volume is inversely proportional to the pressure.

Robert Boyle (1627–1691)   British physicist and chemist who improved the air pump and invented a compressed-air pump; experimented in pneumatics; investigated specific gravities, crystals, and electricity; and discovered the importance of air in propagation of sound. Boyle was one of the first members of a group of scientists that became the Royal Society, and was the author of many technical books including *The Skeptical Chemist* (1661) and *Memoirs for the Natural History of the Human Blood* (1684). His will left a sizable amount of money for lectures in defense of Christianity against unbelievers.

BOYSENBERRY   A large wine-red berry.

Rudolph Boysen   20th-century horticulturist who worked for years crossing loganberries, blackberries, and raspberries. He endured disappointment after disappointment, until one day he found he had discovered a luscious new-tasting berry, which promptly went to market with his name on it.

BRAHMIN   A cultured person from a long-established upper-class family, especially of New England, regarded as haughty or conservative.

Brahma   In Hindu beliefs, the supreme and eternal essence or spirit of the universe; the *Brahmans* make up the highest, priestly Hindu caste.

BRAILLE   A system of printing and writing for the blind.

Louis Braille (1809–1852) French teacher, blind from the age of three. At first he devoted himself to the study of music and was an organist in Paris. In 1828 he began to teach the blind and devised a system of raised-point writing for literature and music which has been widely adopted for instruction of the blind throughout the world.

BRILL'S DISEASE A form of epidemic typhus fever in which the disease recurs years after the original infection.

Nathan Edwin Brill (1860–1948) An American physician, who investigated and was the first to recognize this disease which, as a result, bears his name.

BRINELL TEST A test for determining the relative hardness of metals.

Johann August Brinell (1849–1925) Swedish engineer who, at the Paris International Exposition (1900), introduced the Brinnell machine, an apparatus for measuring the hardness of metals and alloys. It's been in use ever since.

BROBDINGNAGIAN Large, huge.

Brobdingnag A land in Swift's *Gulliver's Travels* inhabited by giants about 60 feet tall.

BRODIE Slang for a suicidal leap.

Steve Brodie (circa 1880s)   The man who jumped off the Brooklyn Bridge on July 23, 1886, but didn't kill himself. There were no witnesses to his leap, but he was fished out of the water under the bridge and said he'd jumped. His name instantly became a synonym for a suicidal dive.

BROUGHAM   A closed, four-wheeled carriage with an open driver's seat.

Henry Brougham (1778–1868)   Scottish jurist and political leader. By the time he was 23 he had started the *Edinburgh Review* and was its most prolific contributor. Brougham took up many causes—the slave trade (he advocated its abolition in 1838), the inhumanity of civil and criminal laws, the savage flogging suffered by soldiers and sailors for the slightest infraction, and censorship of the press. He had an extremely illustrious career, living until the age of 90. However, little of that career is remembered, except for his habit of driving about with Disraeli and Gladstone in a "garden chair on wheels." As they passed, the townsfolk would comment, "There goes Brougham." Pretty soon, "brougham" came to designate the carriage itself, as well as the man.

BROWNIE POINT   Favor gained, as with a superior, for a relatively unimportant act.

Brownies Members of the Girl Scouts in a younger group, six to eight years old. Actually, this group does not earn brownie or merit points as the older Girl Scouts do.

BROWNIAN MOVEMENT The actions of vibratory movement of microscopic particles.

Robert Brown (1773–1858) Scottish botanist who was the naturalist on an expedition to Australia (1801–1805). He collected many new plant species and demonstrated the process described above. Brown was curator of the botanical department in the British Museum in 1827.

BROWNING AUTOMATIC RIFLE, BROWNING MACHINE GUN Rifle widely used in World Wars I and II. The machine gun is capable of firing at more than 500 rounds per minute.

John Moses Browning (1855–1926) The son of a gunsmith; he designed many sporting firearms manufactured by Winchester, Remington, Smith, and Colt Companies. With his brother, Matthew, he organized his own gunmaking firm in 1910 and was highly successful not only with the rifle and machine gun mentioned here, but repeating rifles, automatic pistols, and other firearms.

BRUCELLOSIS Undulant fever.

Sir David Bruce (1855–1931) British physician and bacteriologist, he was a specialist in tropical diseases, the first to describe (1887) the small bacterium that causes undulant fever. He traced the bacterium to the milk of Maltese goats. Bruce traveled widely, served in South Africa (1894–1901), discovered the organism that causes nagana (a disease infecting horses and cattle in tropical Africa caused by the bite of infected tsetse flies), and went to Nyasaland to investigate the connection between human and animal disease.

BRUIN A bear.

Bruin The name of the bear in the medieval epic *Reynard the Fox*, thus the name for a bear in fables and folklore ever since.

BUMBLE or BUMBLEDOM Fussy officialism.

Mr. Bumble A character in Charles Dickens' *Oliver Twist*.

BUNKUM or BUNCOMBE Talk that is empty, insincere, or merely for effect.

Buncombe County, North Carolina The place Congressman Felix Walker, the representative to Congress (1819–1821), referred to when he delivered a long, empty, insincere speech because he felt bound to "make a speech for Buncombe." His name has been long forgotten but the county he represented became famous as a result of his speech, and anything false or done just for effect has forever after been called "buncombe" or "the bunk," for short.

BUNSEN BURNER A small gas burner used in chemistry laboratories.

Robert Wilhelm Eberhard Bunsen (1811–1899) German chemist who was a professor at Heidelberg, spent his life inventing things, not only the Bunsen burner, but the ice calorimeter, a zinc-carbon electric cell (Bunsen cell), a disk photometer which he designed, etc. He also demonstrated the brilliance of flame of magnesium burned in air, formulated (with Roscoe) the reciprocity law, and discovered (with Kirchhoff in 1860) the elements cesium and rubidium.

BUNYANESQUE Large, huge.

Paul Bunyan An imaginary hero supposed to have lived about a hundred years ago in the lumber camps of the northwestern part of the United States. The men who worked in these camps used to sit around their campfires at night and tell "tall tales" about Bunyan and Babe, his great blue ox. Paul was a great giant. Babe, his blue ox, was so big that they said it "measured 42 axe handles and a plug of chewing tobacco between the horns." The character of

Paul Bunyan is probably based on a French-Canadian lumberjack with the same name, who became famous fighting against the English and working in the lumber camps. There are two books about him, both entitled *Paul Bunyan*, one by James Stevens, the other by Esther Shephard.

BURKE   To murder by suffocating.

William Burke (1792–1829)   An Irishman who went about smothering victims in order to sell the bodies for dissection. His accomplice was William Hare. When Burke appeared on the scaffold to be hanged, the crowd of eager watchers yelled, "Burke him, burke him"—meaning smother him as he had smothered others. From then on, his name became associated with murder by suffocation.

BVD's   Men's underwear.

Brandley, Voorhees, and Day   Three men who started the company in 1876 and trademarked their initials as the company's name.

BYZANTINE   In art, designating the decorative style of the mosaics, frescoes, etc. of the Byzantine Empire, characterized by lack of perspective; use of rich colors, especially gold; and emphasis on religious symbolism. In government, characterized by bureaucratic complexity, deviousness, and intrigue.

Byzantine Empire (A.D. 395–1453) Empire in southeast Europe and southwest Asia, formed by the division of the Roman Empire.

C

CAESAR SALAD A popular salad made of romaine lettuce, grated Parmesan cheese, coddled egg, croutons, and other flavorings.

Caesar Gardini (circa 1930) Owner of a restaurant called Caesar's Place in Tijuana, Mexico. One day, so Morris West reports in *Word and Phrase Origins*, more tourists than expected turned up for the bullfights, so Caesar improvised a salad with ingredients which were on hand. The Caesar salad was popularized by Romanoff's restaurant in Hollywood, which added anchovies to the recipe. Others often add bleu or Roquefort cheese. Many others take credit for its creation.

CAESARIAN SECTION A surgical incision through the abdominal wall and uterus performed to extract a fetus.

Julius Caesar (100–44 B.C.) Famous Roman statesman who was said to have been born in this way.

CAIN (usually with raising, as in "raising cain") To create a great disturbance or uproar, make trouble.

Cain The eldest son of Adam and Eve, who killed his brother Abel out of jealousy. (Genesis 4.)

CALIBAN A rude, brutal, contentious person.

Caliban A misshapen monster, son of the witch Sycorax, in Shakespeare's comedy *The Tempest*. Nursing a bitter grudge against Prospero, who has enslaved him and taken possession of the island he considers his own, Caliban makes a ludicrous and unsuccessful attempt to have his master murdered by two shipwrecked drunkards, Stephano and Trinculo. The language of Caliban, which he uses principally to curse his teacher Prospero, is remarkable for its vivid, natural imagery. At the end of the play the repentant Caliban is pardoned by Prospero.

CALICO Any of several kinds of cotton cloth; in England it is unprinted and uncolored, in the U.S., usually printed.

Calicut The former name of Kozhikode, a seaport in India on the Arabian Sea, in the Kerala state. Surprisingly, calico didn't originate in the west, the south, or any place else where it was widely used, but in India, at Calicut, where it was made, and from whence it gets its name.

CALIGULISM Cruelty.

Caligula Gaius Caesar (A.D. *12–41*) He was a Roman emperor (37–41) who was brought up in camps among soldiers. His nickname was Caligula because in youth he wore *caligae,* which means "little boots" or "military boots." He delighted in torture and bloodshed and his reign was marked by extreme cruelty and tyranny. Many historians consider Caligula to have been insane. He was finally murdered by members of the Praetorian Guard led by Chaerea.

CALLIOPE Instrument like an organ having a series of steam whistles.

Kalliope or Calliope In Greek mythology, the Muse of eloquence and epic poetry, often called "the beautiful-voiced."

CALVINISM Religious doctrines which emphasize the omnipotence of God, the sinfulness of man, and the salvation of the elect by God's grace alone. A rigid moral code.

John Calvin (*1509–1564*) French theologian (whose original name was John Chauvin or Caulvin), he was banished from Paris in 1533 and took up residence in Switzerland where he published books outlining his credo. His zeal and his copious writings brought together a doctrine known as *Calvinism* which stated the religious opinions of Calvin and his followers.

CAMELLIA Any of several shrubs or trees of the genus *Camellia*, native to Asia, having evergreen leaves and showy, variously-colored flowers.

George Joseph Kamel or Camel (1661–1706) Jesuit missionary who was sent to the Philippine Islands from his native Moravia where he made a special study of minerals, animals, and plants. He was the first to identify and describe this flower, also known as Japonica, to the great botanist Linnaeus, who named it in his honor.

CANTER A smooth, easy pace like a moderate gallop.

Canter A clipped form of Canterbury, coined from the easy-going pace of the horses ridden by pilgrims paying homage to the tomb of St. Thomas à Becket in Canterbury, a city in Kent, England. These pilgrims were immortalized in the poetic imagination of Geoffrey Chaucer in the *Canterbury Tales*, an unfinished literary work consisting of stories told by pilgrims on their way to Canterbury.

CARDIGAN A sweater or knitted jacket opening down the front.

The 7th Earl of Cardigan, James Thomas Brudenell (1797–1868) A distinguished English soldier and member of Parliament (1818–1829) who entered the army in 1824. He became commander of cavalry and led the "Six Hundred" in the famous charge of the Light Brigade, in the battle of Balaklava in the Crimean War in 1854. He was the first man to reach the Russian lines. In 1861 he became a lieutenant general. It was during his years in the cavalry that he longed for—and finally had made for him—a less confining garment than was traditionally worn, a sweater which opened down the front and could be buttoned up or not as comfort dictated. It quickly became popular in army and civilian circles and was thereafter known as the cardigan.

CASANOVA A romantic or promiscuous man, a libertine.

Giovanni Jacopo Casanova de Seingalt (1725–1798) An Italian adventurer who, surprisingly, was educated for the priesthood. Later, he was expelled for scandalous conduct from the Seminary of St. Cyprian. In turn Casanova became a preacher, abbé, alchemist, cabalist, gambler, violin player, librarian (for Count von Waldstein at Dux Castle in Bohemia), and seducer of women. He bragged about his prowess and claimed to have bedded thousands of willing ladies. Nevertheless (or maybe because of his reputation) he became a friend of the great, including the pope (who bestowed upon him the papal order of the Golden Spur). Among his other friends were Empress Catherine, Voltaire, von Haller, Mme. de Pompadour, and Cagliostro. He traveled to Russia, where he was forced to flee because of a scandal and a duel. Giovanni went from one scrape to another, and wrote of his adventures (mostly sexual) in *Memoires Ecrits Par Lui-Même* (12 volumes), a cynical and clever record of his rogueries and life.

CASHMERE Fine, downy wool growing beneath the outer hair of the cashmere goat.

Kashmir The Himalayan regions of India and Tibet, where cashmere or kashmir goats are raised and highly prized for the wool they bear.

CASLON A style of type.

William Caslon (1692–1766) An English type founder; he produced a style of type excelling in legibility, which was used in England and America and on the Continent until about 1800. The Chiswick Press revived Caslon type about 1843 and it has been in popular use ever since.

CASSANDRA Anyone who utters unheeded prophecies.

Cassandra In Greek mythology, a daughter of Priam, King of Troy, endowed with the gift of prophecy but fated by Apollo never to be believed.

CASTLE WALK A dance.

Vernon Blythe Castle (1887–1918) American dancer, who, with his wife Irene, formed the most popular dancing couple of the time (circa 1912). Castle originated the one-step, turkey trot, and the Castle walk. An aviator in the Royal Flying Corps, he was killed in an aviation accident in Ft. Worth, Texas, on Feb. 15, 1918.

CATCHPENNY   Fraudulent.

Christopher Cat   Eighteenth-century English tavern-keeper of "The Cat and the Fiddle" in London who is credited with being the inspiration for "catchpenny" or "fraudulent." Whether he cheated his customers isn't known. What is known is that his tavern was the meeting place for the Kit-Kat Club, a social club for Whigs, the ruling political party of the time.

CATHERINE WHEEL   A firework similar to a pinwheel.

St. Catherine of Alexandria (d. A.D. 307)   Christian virgin and martyr, who was beheaded after a failed attempt to torture her on a spiked wheel.

CATO   To censor.

Marcus Porcius Cato (95–46 B.C.)   Known as "Cato the Censor" and "Cato the Elder," a Roman statesman and censor who endeavored to restore by legislation what he believed to be the high morals and simplicity of life characteristic of the early days of the republic. He was not successful.

CELSIUS   A system for measuring temperature where "0" stands for freezing, and 100 is the boiling point of water.

Anders Celsius   Swedish astronomer, a professor at Uppsala, and builder and director of an observatory there; he published many collections on the aurora borealis. He was a member of a French expedition to measure the degree of meridian in polar regions in 1736, advocated the introduction of the Gregorian calendar, and was the first to describe the centigrade thermometer, now properly called the Celsius thermometer.

CEREAL   An edible grain, such as wheat, oats, or corn.

Ceres   In Roman mythology, the goddess of agriculture.

CHAMPAGNE   An effervescent white wine.

Champagne   A region and former province of France. Only wine produced in this region was thought to be worthy of the name "champagne," but today any bubbling white wine produced there or elsewhere is called by this name and stands as a symbol of luxurious living. (See DOM PERIGNON.)

CHAPLINESQUE   Humorous.

   Charles Chaplin (1889–1977)   Motion picture actor born in London, he was onstage from childhood. He brought his vaudeville act to America and achieved world-wide renown as a comedian after making his motion picture debut in 1914. Among the many motion pictures he produced and starred in are *A Dog's Life, The Kid, The Circus, The Gold Rush, City Lights, Modern Times, The Great Dictator,* etc.

CHARCOT'S DISEASE   Multiple sclerosis.

   Jean Martin Charcot (1825–1893)   Professor of pathological anatomy in Paris, and a physician at the Salpetriere from 1862, where he established a neurological clinic known for its work on hysteria and hypnotism, sclerosis (subsequently named Charcot's disease) and senile diseases, etc.

CHARLATAN   Someone who pretends to have knowledge or skill that he does not have; a quack.

   Dr. A. M. Latan   A famous quack dentist who used to tour Paris (circa 1840) in a magnificent car, in which he had a traveling dispensary. A man blowing a horn went ahead to announce his approach.

Sightseers used to cry out in delight, "Voilà, le char de Latan," *char* meaning car.

CHARLEY MORE   The British Navy's synonym for everything upright, honest, reasonable.

Charley More (circa 1840)   A Maltese publican who had a huge sign-board over his house of refreshment on which was flamboyantly inscribed: "Charley More—the Fair Thing." It caught the eyes of naval men and the name was admitted into their vocabulary as the pinnacle of truth and integrity. "Come on, act Charley More" was, and is, an appeal to man's sense of fair play.

CHARNOCKITE   Any of a series of rocks ranging from granite to nonite.

John Charnock (d. 1693)   The English founder of Calcutta. He moved the East India Company factory from Hooghly, which was besieged, to the island at the mouth of the Ganges in 1686. His tombstone is made of charnockite, which was named for him. Small and rather late recognition for a man of accomplishment.

CHARTREUSE   A liqueur.

La Grande Chartreuse   A monastery near Grenoble where the Carthusian monks originally made the drink.

CHASSEPOT A breech-loading rifle used by the French army between 1866 and 1874.

A.A. Chassepot (1833–1905) A French inventor, born in Bas-rhin, who invented the musket called after him.

CHATEAUBRIAND A double-thick center cut of tenderloin steak.

François-René de Chateaubriand (1768–1848) An eminent French writer and statesman who lived to the ripe old age of 80. But his name is probably remembered more today for his chef's achievements rather than his own. The renowned Monmirel invented for ambassadorial dinners the gastronomic delight that the chef named "beefsteak Chateaubriand," and which he undoubtedly served to King George IV when the king dined there, as he often did.

CHAUVINISM Unreasoning devotion to one's country, ethnic group, race, or sex, with contempt for those who are not members of the preferred group.

Nicolas Chauvin A legendary French soldier of Revolutionary and Napoleonic times, whose unreasoning devotion and enthusiasm for Napoleon were so exaggerated that his comrades finally started to ridicule him. From his name the word *chauvinism* is said to be derived.

CHESHIRE CAT   A grinning cat.

   Cheshire Cat   In *Alice's Adventures in Wonderland* by Lewis Carroll, a grinning cat that gradually disappeared until only its grin remained visible.

CHESTERFIELD   A single-breasted or double-breasted overcoat with a velvet collar.

   The 19th Earl of Chesterfield   The earl credited with having his tailor design a coat to his specifications—the Chesterfield. Whether he did or not is moot because there were several holders of the title during the 19th century when it was created. What is known is that some unsung and unremembered tailor to one of the Chesterfields designed, cut, and sewed the coat.

CHIANTI   A dry red wine.

   Mount Chianti   A region in Italy where this wine is produced.

CHICKEN TETRAZZINI   Diced chicken in cream sauce, flavored with sherry and baked in a casserole with thin spaghetti, cheese, and mushrooms.

   Luisa Tetrazzini (1872–1941)   Italian-born diva whose role of Lucia di Lammermoor made her famous to opera lovers throughout the world.

CHIHUAHUA   A very small dog with pointed ears and a smooth coat.

Chihuahua   A state of Mexico in the northeast where these tiny dogs originated.

CHIMERA   An impossible or foolish fancy.

Chimera   In Greek mythology, a fire-breathing monster usually represented as having a lion's head, a goat's body, and a serpent's tail, killed by Bellerophon from the back of Pegasus. Also *chimaera*, a genus of fishes related to the sharks.

CHINA   Porcelain, any earthenware dishes or crockery.

China   All porcelain was originally made in China, and imported from that country.

CHIPPENDALE   A style of furniture characterized by graceful lines and, often, rococo ornamentation.

Thomas Chippendale (1718–1779)   English cabinetmaker, son of a Yorkshire carver and maker of picture frames. He established a factory in London in 1749 and published *The Gentleman and Cabinet Maker's Director* in 1754, which was a folio of furniture designs exemplifying his characteristic solid, but graceful and ornate, style.

CHISHOLM TRAIL   A former cattle trail from San Antonio, Texas to Abilene, Kansas.

Jesse Chisholm (1806–1868)   Trader who drove his wagon over the trail, and the wheels left marks in the grass and ruts in the earth to mark the way. Jesse's father was a Scotsman and his mother a Cherokee Indian. He was born in Tennessee and never was a cattleman or cowboy, but his trail showed that it was possible to drive the great herds of Texas longhorn cattle to market, on the hoof, all the way up from the Rio Grande. He and his trail are immortalized in the folk song, "The Old Chisholm Trail."

CHRISTY   A ski turn.

Christiania   The former name of Oslo, Norway, where *christianias* or *christys* were popularized.

CICERONE   A guide who conducts sightseers.

Marcus Tullius Cicero (106–43 b.c.)   Roman orator, statesman and philosopher, known for his many battles and orations but not for encouraging tourism. Therefore it is not known why he's lent his name to a tourist guide, except that the guide's loquacity might match Cicero's.

CIMMERIAN   Gloomy, dark.

Cimmerian   One of a mythical people described by Homer as inhabiting a land of perpetual darkness.

CINCHONA   Any of various trees of the genus *Cinchona* whose bark yields quinine and other medicines.

The Countess of Chincón   Francisca Henriques de Ribera (1576–1639), who introduced it into Europe after recovering from a fever by using the cinchona bark.

CINDERELLA   Any girl who achieves recognition or affluence after a period of obscurity and neglect.

Cinderella   The fairy-tale heroine who escapes from a life of drudgery and marries a handsome prince through the intervention of a fairy godmother.

CIRCE   A siren or alluring female.

Circe   An enchantress described in the *Odyssey* who detains Odysseus for a year and turns his men into swine.

CLARKIA   Any of a genus of American wildflowers of the evening primrose family having rosy or purple flowers.

William Clark (1770–1838)   An American explorer who engaged in frontier service against the Indians. With Capt. Meriwether Lewis, he led an expedition to find a route to the Pacific Ocean (Lewis and Clark expedition). Governor of Missouri

Territory (1813–1821), he discovered the delightful wildflower, the Clarkia.

CLARENCE   A four-wheeled carriage with seats for four persons.

The Duke of Clarence (*1765–1837*)   Later, William IV of England, also called "the Sailor-King" and "Silly Billy." As a midshipman, he served in action off Cape St. Vincent in 1780 and was captain of a frigate in 1785. He sat in the House of Lords and opposed emancipation of slaves. His mistress was the actress Dorothea Jordan. He was forced to break off this affair to marry Adelaide of Saxe-Meningen (1818) and he became heir to the throne and Lord High Admiral in 1827. He succeeded George IV as king in 1830 and was in turn followed on the British throne by his niece Victoria.

CLAYTONIA   Any of a genus (*Claytonia*) of small, spring-flowering plants of the purslane family, with white and rose-colored flowers.

John Clayton (*1693–1773*)   English botanist who moved to Virginia in 1705 and supplied specimens used by Gronovius, a leading Dutch botanist of the time, for inclusion in *Flora Virginica*, which was published in two parts in 1743 and *Flora Orientalis* published in 1755. Among the specimens Clayton sent to Holland was the genus described above.

CLERIHEW   A humorous quatrain about a person who is generally named in the first line.

Edmund Clerihew Bentley (1875–1956)   A journalist at the *Daily News* and *Daily Telegraph* in England who amused himself in the evenings by dashing off quatrains. One of his most famous is about a well-known architect:

> Sir Christopher Wren
> Said "I am going to dine with some men.
> If anybody calls
> Say I am designing St. Paul's."

He published them as "clerihews." He also wrote the celebrated detective novel *Trent's Last Case*. A quarter of a century later, he wrote two more, *Trent's Own Case* and *Trent Intervenes*.

CLEVELAND   A city in northeastern Ohio, a port and industrial center on Lake Erie.

Moses Cleaveland (1754–1806)   American pioneer who was an official of the Connecticut Land Company. He was sent to the west to survey and settle land bought by the company. From all accounts, he was just an ordinary nine-to-five working man who wanted nothing more than to get home in time to hear the 9 o'clock news, as told by the town crier. Nevertheless, he became famous by founding (1796) Cleveland, Ohio, which was first called Cleaveland. He really did nothing to earn the honor, except to survey some land. The "a" in the original name was later removed to make the town name fit in a newspaper headline.

CLOTH Fabric or material formed by weaving, knitting, etc.

Clotho In Greek mythology, one of the three Fates, spinner of the thread of destiny.

COCKER, ACCORDING TO Strictly correct.

Edward Cocker (1631–75) Author of a popular arithmetic book, which ran into 60 editions and was considered the acme of correctness. "According to Cocker" means to be 100% accurate, as he and his book were.

COINTREAU A trademark for a sweet, orange-flavored, colorless liqueur.

Cointreau Family The name of the French family of wine producers who first produced this liqueur.

COLINSIA Any of various North American plants of the genus *Colinsia* having blue-and-white or purplish flowers.

Zaccheus Collins (1764–1831) American botanist; the first to identify this flower of the new world and to bring it to the attention of the world's botanists.

COLLINS   A tall iced drink made of gin, vodka, rum or other liquor, lemon or lime juice, carbonated water, and sugar.

Tom Collins   A bartender with this name who supposedly invented the drink.

COLOGNE   A scented liquid made of alcohol and various fragrant oils.

Cologne, Germany   City on the west bank of the Rhine where "eau de cologne" or "water of cologne" was first made.

COLOSSAL   Enormous in size, extent, or degree; tremendous.

Colossus of Rhodes   A huge statue, 120 feet high, of Apollo, built about 280 B.C. It was formerly set at the entrance to the harbor of ancient Rhodes.

COLT   A trademark for a type of revolver.

Samuel Colt (1814–1862)   Inventor of this trademarked revolver, which is sometimes called the gun that won the West. Colt's patent for the revolver was issued in 1836. In 1839 and 1850 he applied for and received patents for two improved models. The revolver, which could fire six bullets without having to be reloaded, was one of the most important weapons used in the West against the Indians. Colt's invention, with a few improvements, is still used today.

COLUMBIAN Of or pertaining to the United States.

Christopher Columbus (1451–1506) Italian explorer in the service of Spain who, in 1492, discovered America, and lent his name to all sorts of places and things, including columbine, a plant; columbium, the element named after him because it was discovered in the United States (in Connecticut); columbite, a black mineral, etc.

COMEDY A play, motion picture, or other work that is humorous in its treatment.

Comus A classical deity of revelry. (Latin, from Greek *komos*, meaning revel, festival procession.)

COMPTON EFFECT Changes in wave lengths of scattered X-rays.

Arthur Holly Compton (1892–1962) Nobel prize winner for physics in 1927. He investigated the earth's rotation, and discovered the change in wave lengths of scattered X-rays known as the *Compton Effect.* He shared the Nobel with C. T. R. Wilson. Compton was chancellor of Washington University, St. Louis, from 1945 until his death.

COMSTOCK LODE A very rich mine discovered in 1859 in Nevada.

H. T. Comstock (1820–1870) A prospector in the American West, he was born in Canada. He was successful, but didn't benefit from his discovery. In Nevada he discovered a very rich vein of gold and silver, a mine which he instantly named the "Comstock Lode." He sold his claim for a small amount, and got none of the riches which the mine spewed forth until the veins ran out, circa 1890.

COMSTOCKERY Overzealous censorship of literature and other arts because of alleged immorality.

Anthony Comstock (1844–1915) American reformer and crusader against vice. He founded and was the secretary for the Society for the Suppression of Vice and conducted spectacular raids on publishers and vendors. He is the author of *Frauds Exposed*, *Traps for the Young*, and *Morals Versus Art*.

COMTISM Positivism.

Auguste Comte (1798–1857) French mathematician and philosopher and the founder of positivism, a theory of perception and the nature of reality. Unfortunately Comte died insane. This put a blight on comtism, and it floundered.

CONDOM A sheath, usually made of thin rubber, designed to cover the penis during sexual intercourse to prevent venereal disease or conception.

Dr. Condom or Conton A doctor so named is popularly supposed to be the inventor of the sheath, although according to the Oxford English Dictionary "no 18th-century English physician has been traced." It's probable that this contraceptive device *was* invented by a doctor, and it's also likely that he or his patients called it after him; however, this can't be proved. What is known about the condom is that it was first introduced circa 1700 in England.

CONFUCIANISM An ethical system emphasizing personal virtue, devotion to family (including the spirits of one's ancestors), and justice.

Confucius (551–479 B.C.) Chinese philosopher and teacher whose original name was Kung Chiu, and long known in China as Kung Fu-tse. Not a religious teacher, his precepts dealt with morals, the family system, social reforms, and statecraft. His maxims are still taught as a guide for daily life. (One of his most famous: "What I do not wish men to do to me, I also wish not to do to men.") He called himself a "transmitter, not an originator."

COOK'S TOUR Any guided sightseeing or inspection tour.

Thomas Cook (1808–1892) The founder of Thomas Cook & Son in England, he aided visitors to reach the Great Exhibition of 1851, the Paris Exhibition in 1855, and to make a circular tour of Europe in 1856. He initiated the system of providing hotel accommodations as well as travel tickets. In 1884 he was commissioned to convey General Gordon to the Sudan.

COPERNICAN SYSTEM   The theory that the planets revolve around the sun and that the turning of the earth on its axis accounts for the apparent rising and setting of the stars; basis of modern astronomy.

Nicolaus Copernicus (1473–1543)   Polish astronomer who lectured on astronomy at Rome in 1500. He probably began consideration of his theory of the solar system as early as 1507. His great work, *De revolutionibus orbium coelestium*, was practically completed circa 1530 but he delayed printing it because of political and religious conditions. The printing was completed in 1543 just in time to reach Copernicus on his deathbed. He is regarded as the founder of modern astronomy.

COULOMB   A unit of electrical charge equal to the quantity of charge transferred in one second by a steady current of one ampere.

Charles Augustin de Coulomb (1736–1806) French physicist known for his work on friction, and especially on electricity and magnetism. Coulomb's law showed that the electrical charge is on the surface of a conductor.

COVENTRY, SEND TO   To refuse to associate with, ostracize.

Coventry, England   An industrial city of central Warwickshire, England, where Royalist prisoners were sent at the time of Charles I (1600–1649). Under Charles I, son of James I, civil war broke out. Charles was beheaded in 1649, and the Puritans set up a republican government called the Commonwealth, with Puritan leader Oliver Cromwell ruling as Lord Protector.

COWPER'S GLANDS   A pair of small glands with ducts opening into the male urethra.

William Cowper (1666–1709)   London surgeon and anatomist who discovered and described the glands. He was fascinated with what *wasn't known* about the human body and set about learning all he could, and shared that knowledge with the world. He wrote *The Anatomy of the Humane* (sic) *Body* in 1698, thereby filling many gaps in medical knowledge.

CRAP   Bodily excretions; nonsense, falseness, insincerity; something useless, inferior, worthless; trash; junk—also CRAPPY.

Thomas Crapper (1837–1910)   A Victorian English engineer, he is responsible for inventing the valve and siphon arrangement that made modern flush toilets possible. To flush their toilets the Victorians simply pulled a chain that lifted a valve that released water from a cistern into a flush pipe. Since the valves rarely had a snug fit, the water in most toilets flowed ceaselessly. In the 1870s the British Board of Trade sent out a call for a more efficient system—and Crapper, a Chelsea sanitary engineer, answered the call. His solution, still observable today, depends upon a float, a metal arm, and a siphonic action to empty the reservoir. His method passed a critical public test in a demonstration at the Health Exhibition of 1884, and rapidly came into general use. Such a breakthrough earned Crapper a royal commission to install the facilities in Edward VII's new country home in Sandringham. At least one testimony to Thomas Crapper's memory remains in London. It can be found in the Westminster Abbey cloisters among the tombstones of England's most celebrated—the inscription "Thos. Crapper, sanitary engineer, Chelsea" is still a clearly visible inscription on top of a manhole cover.

CRÊPES SUZETTE A thin dessert pancake sweetened and served with an orange or tangerine sauce and flaming brandy.

Suzette The woman who accompanied Edward, Prince of Wales, the son of Queen Victoria, to the Café de Paris in Monte Carlo (circa 1865). Chef Henri Charpentier, who had created the dish on the spot, was asked by the prince to name it after "Suzette." Charpentier had originally planned to call his new dessert "Crêpes Princesse." Many chefs take credit for inventing this dish, but Charpentier tells this story in his cookbook.

CRETONNE A heavy, unglazed cotton, linen or rayon fabric, colorfully printed and used for draperies and slipcovers.

Creton A village in Normandy, France, where the material known as cretonne was first made.

CRICHTON, AN ADMIRABLE An outstanding and highly-principled man.

The Admirable Crichton A real person, as well as a character in James M. Barrie's play of the same name, first performed in 1902. The real-life Crichton was born in 1560, an outstanding physical and mental prodigy. By the age of fifteen he had mastered a dozen languages and was knowledgeable in all the known sciences. In France he dazzled the outstanding students and faculty of the Sorbonne. After several years serving with the French Army, he traveled to Italy where he became a tutor to sons of dukes and princes, impressing everyone with his looks, brilliance, and agility as a swordsman. He died in his early twenties, having been as foolish as any other man in attempting to steal the love of a prince's lady. He was promptly assaulted by three masked men and expired on the spot.

CROCUS   Any of a large genus (*Crocus*) of spring-blooming plants of the iris family, with yellow, purple, or white flowers.

   Crocus   In Greek mythology, a youth called "the lover."

CROW, JIM   Discrimination against or segregation of Afro-Americans.

   Thomas "Jim Crow" Rice (*circa 1820*)   A white man who appeared in blackface. His song and dance went like this: "Wheel about, turn about, do just so. Every time I wheel about, I jump Jim Crow." The act was a great success and the expression came to symbolize for the American black every form of discrimination imposed upon him. For more than a century expressions such as "Jim Crow laws" and "Jim Crow schools" were widely used.

CURIE   The unit used in measuring radioactivity.

   Marie Curie (*1867–1934*)   Polish chemist and physicist in France, she discovered polonium and radium (1898) in collaboration with her husband, Pierre. She and Pierre were awarded the Nobel Prize in physics in 1903 and in chemistry in 1911.

CYCLOPEAN   Huge, gigantic, enormous.

   Cyclops   In Greek mythology, any of the three one-eyed Titans who forged thunderbolts for Zeus.

Also, any of a race of one-eyed giants, reputedly descended from these Titans, inhabiting the island of Sicily.

CYRILLIC ALPHABET An old Slavic alphabet, currently used in modified form for Russian, other languages of the Soviet Union, Bulgarian, and other Slavic languages.

St. Cyril (**A.D. 827–869**) Greek Christian missionary, who, with his brother Saint Methodius, is regarded as the inventor of the Cyrillic alphabet.

D

DAEDAL Skillfully made, ingenious.

Daedalus In Greek myth, the skillful artist and builder of the Labyrinth in Crete, and fabricator of wings used by him and his son Icarus to escape from imprisonment in the Labyrinth.

DAGUERREOTYPE An early photographic process.

Louis Jacques-Mandé Daguerre (**1789–1851**) A scene-painter for the opera who spent his life working on "the obtaining of permanent pictures on metal plates by the action of sunlight." His work led to the discovery of the daguerreotype process, which in turn led to modern photography.

DAKIN'S SOLUTION A surgical disinfectant.

Henry Drysdale Dakin (1880–1952) An English chemist, he developed his solution during World War I. He is also known for his researches in biochemistry, especially on enzymes. He was awarded the Davy medal by the Royal Society in 1941.

DALMATIAN A dog of a breed having a short, smooth white coat covered with black or dark-brown spots. Also called "coach dog," "carriage dog."

Dalmatia A region of Croatia, Yugoslavia, along the eastern coast of the Adriatic Sea where these dogs were first bred.

DAMASK A rich, patterned fabric of cotton, linen, silk, or wool.

Damascus The capital of Syria, an ancient city in the southwestern part of the country, where *damasks* were created.

DAMOCLES, SWORD OF Any imminent danger.

Damocles A courtier of ancient Syracuse who, according to legend, was given a lesson in the perils of a ruler's life when the king seated him at a feast under a sword hanging by a single hair.

DARBY & JOAN   An old married couple, much devoted to each other.

Darby & Joan   The title of an 18th-century song which celebrated just such a pair.

DARDAN   A Trojan.

Dardanus   In Greek mythology, the eponymous hero of the Dardans and founder of Troy.

DARWIN TULIP   A type of garden tulip having squarish flowers in a wide variety of colors.

Charles Darwin (1809–1882)   British naturalist who expounded the theory of evolution by natural selection in his famous book *The Origin of the Species* (1859). The flower is named to honor him.

DAVENPORT   A large sofa, often convertible into a bed; a small desk (British).

Davenport   19th-century furniture maker of whom little is known, except that he was creative and skillful.

DAVIS CUP   A trophy awarded to the nation whose team is the winner of the International Lawn Tennis Championship.

Dwight F. Davis (1879–1945)   An American civic leader and government official, he donated the cup in 1900. Davis was U.S. secretary of war from 1925–

1929, governor general of the Philippines from 1929–1932, and director general of the U.S. Army Specialists Corps in 1942.

DAVY LAMP   An early safety lamp for miners.

Sir Humphrey Davy (1778–1829)   A professor of chemistry at the Royal Institution in London. He made many discoveries besides inventing the Davy lamp. He was the first to discover the exhilarating effect of nitrous oxide (laughing gas) when inhaled, and the first to prepare potassium, sodium, and calcium by electrolytic means. Michael Faraday was his assistant. (See FARAD.)

DELILAH   A seductive woman, temptress.

Delilah   In the Bible, a Philistine woman who betrayed Samson, her lover, to the Philistines by having his hair shorn as he slept thus depriving him of his strength. (Judges 16.) (See SAMSON).

DELPHIC   Obscure in meaning, ambiguous.

Delphic Oracle   The Oracle of the Greek god Apollo at Delphi. In the temple of Apollo there was a crack in the floor just over a stream of water called the Cassotis. A woman prophet seated herself over this crack, from which steam rose. The vapors were supposed to send her into a trance, during which she spoke the word of Apollo. The priest took down her words, and then interpreted them. Frequently the words and the interpretations were sketchy, to say the least. (See PYTHIAN.)

DELSARTE SYSTEM A system of calisthenics combined with singing and acting and dancing to develop bodily poise and grace.

François Delsarte (1811–1871) French teacher of singing and dramatics who became world famous (during his time!) for his system of combining exercise with dramatics. His students swore he enabled them to develop not only coordination, but power and grace.

DEMOCRITEAN An advocate of Democritus's ideas.

Democritus (460?–370? B.C.) Greek philosopher, exponent of atomism, which holds that the universe is made up of tiny, simple, indivisible particles that cannot be destroyed or divided. He was correct, except for the fact that the atom can be divided.

DENIM A coarse twilled cloth used for overalls and work uniforms.

Nimes City in southern France made famous throughout the world for its coarse *de nimes* (denim) cloth.

DERBY A horse race for three-year-olds held annually at Epsom Downs in Surrey, England.

The 12th Earl of Derby, Edward Smith Stanley I (1752–1834) Nobleman who instituted the race. Epsom Downs did not really become a major sporting center until the 12th Earl of Derby came of age and took over the family estates, The Oaks. The Earl entertained lavishly during the racing season, which was always the same—with races for mature horses run for either two or four miles. For the sake of variety, the Earl proposed a race for three-year-old fillies over a shorter distance. It was enthusiastically cheered when it was first run in 1780. There was already a race called "The Oaks" so someone suggested the new race be called the "Derby." It stuck. The races at Epsom became more fashionable than ever, and the house parties at The Oaks more lavish.

DERRICK A large crane for hoisting and moving heavy objects.

Thomas Derrick A famous hangman during the reigns of Elizabeth and James I (circa 1600). It is said that Derrick executed the unfortunate Earl of Essex in 1601, in spite of the fact that Essex had saved his life years before when Derrick was condemned to death for rape in Calais. That fact is not clear, but what is clear is that Derrick expedited the deaths of well over three thousand people during

71

his long years of service at Tyburn. The device used to support a hangman's noose and a derrick are similarly shaped, and the word "derrick" was originally applied to a gallows.

DERRINGER   A short-barreled pistol with a large bore.

Henry Deringer (1806–1868)   A gunsmith who started out in the gun trade by making squirrel rifles which he traded for lumber with the Delaware River boatmen in the early 19th century. In the 1840s he designed and crafted a little box-lock pocket pistol called the deringer, spelled with one "r." They quickly became popular with everyone from Philadelphia politicians to Gold Rush prospectors. The demand far exceeded the supply and imitations began to appear. A French imitation appeared signed "Derringer" with two "r's." In spite of the competition, demand for the real thing increased and Deringer was soon operating one of the country's largest armories. One of his guns was used by John Wilkes Booth at the Ford Theatre on Good Friday, 1865, to assassinate President Abraham Lincoln. Oddly enough, the misspelling of his name—with two instead of one "r"—is retained to this day.

DEUS EX MACHINA   Any unexpected, artificial, or improbable character, device, or event suddenly introduced to resolve a situation or untangle a plot.

Deus ex Machina   A deity in Greek and Roman drama who was brought in by stage machinery to intervene in a difficult situation. The name literally means "God from a machine."

DEUTZIA   Any of a genus of shrubs of the saxifrage family bearing many white flowers in the spring.

Jean Deutz   An 18th-century Dutch flower fancier who particularly admired the Deutzia and called it to the attention of gardeners and botanists worldwide.

DEWAR FLASK   An insulated container used to store gases.

Sir James Dewar (1842–1923)   Scottish chemist and physicist, professor of philosophy at Cambridge and later, of chemistry at the Royal Institution, London. He invented the Dewar vessel, forerunner of the thermos bottle, and with F. A. Abel, invented cordite.

DEWEY DECIMAL SYSTEM   A system of book classification for libraries.

Melvil Dewey (1851–1931)   Librarian who first proposed the system in 1876 while serving as the librarian at Amherst College. It's now used by the majority of libraries everywhere. Dewey also was the founder and editor of the *Library Journal* (1876–1881) and *Library Notes* (1886–1898), as well as founder of the American Library Association.

DICK TEST   A test to determine scarlet fever.

George Dick (1881–1967)   With his wife, isolated the germ of, and originated a serum for, scarlet fever. He's best known for devising the test which determines susceptibility to scarlet fever.

DIDO   A mischievous trick, prank, caper.

Dido   In Roman mythology, the founder and queen of Carthage. She lends her name to pranks and tricks because of the story that Dido, on being allowed to purchase as much land as might be covered with the hide of a bull, ordered the hide cut into thin strips, with which she surrounded a large area.

DISCORD   To fail to agree or harmonize; to clash.

Discordia   The Roman goddess of strife.

DOBERMAN PINSCHER   A breed of large dogs with smooth dark hair and tan markings.

Ludwig Dobermann (circa 1890)   German dog breeder.

DOBRO   A trademark for a type of acoustic guitar with an aluminum resonator used in country music.

Dopera Brothers   Brothers who used the first two letters of their name and the first three letters of "brothers" to name their invention, which they developed in 1928. They were also influenced to use the name *dobro* because it means "good" in the Czech language.

DR. FELL   Famous irreverent rhyme.

Dr. John Fell   A 17th-century dean of Christ Church, Oxford. Dr. Fell was immortalized because he expelled one of his students, a wit named Tom Brown. After an argument, Fell agreed to remit the ouster if Brown would translate a Latin epigram. The Latin epigram he was asked to translate actually read: "I do not love thee, nor can I tell why, but this much I can tell you, I do not love you." Brown is reported to have improvised this version of that epigram on the spot: "I do not like thee, Doctor Fell, The reason why I cannot tell, but this I know, and I know full well, I do not like thee, Doctor Fell." When he graduated from college Brown wrote many verses but his most famous is the one beginning "I do not like thee, Doctor Fell," which has been said about many unwitting doctors ever since.

DOILY   A small, ornamental mat made of lace, linen, or the like, and used to protect or adorn furniture.

Mr. Doily or Doyley (first name unknown) A 17th-century London linen-draper; he had a shop on the Strand during the reign of Queen Anne. He became prosperous by selling various summer fabrics trimmed with embroidery or crochet work, and, being a good businessman, used up the remnants by making ornamental mats for the table called "doilies."

DOLBY A trademark for a device used in tape recording and broadcasting that reduces electronic background noise and improves sound quality.

R. Dolby (1933–) U.S. recording engineer who invented the device.

DOLOMITE A common rock-forming mineral, often occurring in extensive beds.

Déodat Guy Silvain Tancrède Gratet de Dolomieu (1750–1801) An extraordinary French geologist and mineralogist, who had rock-like strength of character. He was the scientist on Bonaparte's expedition to Egypt in 1798; on the return trip, he was captured and imprisoned at Messina for 21 months. While in prison, he made a pen of wood and, using soot from the lamp, wrote on the margins of his Bible *Traite de Philosophie Mineralogique* and *Memoir Sur l'Espèce Minerale,* two important books on minerals. After his release, he was professor of mineralogy at the Museum of Natural History, Paris.

DOM PÉRIGNON   A fine champagne.

Dom Pierre Pérignon (1638–1715)   A blind man who joined the Benedictine order in France and was put in charge of the vineyards. His fantastic sense of taste and smell enabled him to experiment in improving the vines he attended, and he is credited with having invented champagne and, in fact, all sparkling wines. (See CHAMPAGNE.)

DON JUAN   A libertine, philanderer, rake.

Don Juan Tenorio   14th-century Spanish aristocrat who embodied all the character traits of his numerous namesakes, who is portrayed in many poems, plays, and operas as a no-good philanderer, which apparently Tenorio was.

DONNYBROOK   A rough, rowdy fight or free-for-all.

Donnybrook Fair   A former yearly fair at Donnybrook, near Dublin, Ireland, noted for its excessive brawling.

DOPPLER EFFECT   The apparent change of frequency of sound waves or light waves, varying with the relative velocity of the source and observer.

Christian Doppler (1803–1853)   Austrian physicist and mathematician and the first to enunciate the principle that if the distance is changing between an observer and a source of constant vibrations, as of sound or light, the wave appears to be greater or lesser than the true value—according to the distance being diminished or lengthened. In other words, the apparent nature of things changes as it is observed. This was an important discovery in 1842.

DOUBTING THOMAS   A person who habitually doubts; a chronic skeptic.

St. Thomas, the Apostle   A disciple of Jesus who, according to the Bible, expressed skepticism about Christ's resurrection. After Christ appeared before him and convinced him, Christ said: "Thomas, because thou hast seen me, thou hast believed; blessed are they that have not seen, and yet have believed." In other words, have faith.

DOUGLAS FIR   A tall evergreen timber tree.

David Douglas (1798–1834)   Scottish botanist appointed to collect specimens in the United States for the Royal Horticultural Society in 1823. On a later expedition in America and the Pacific he discovered the Douglas fir (1825). The Douglas squirrel is also named for him.

DOVER'S POWDER   A powdered drug made essentially of opium and ipecac, used to reduce pain and induce vomiting.

Thomas Dover (1660–1742) An adventurer, and also a doctor. He was the captain of a privateer, a ship privately owned and manned but authorized by a government during wartime to attack and capture enemy vessels. The ship was commanded by the famous Woodes Rogers. Together, Dover and Rogers and the crew of the ship sacked and looted Guayaquil in Peru (now in Ecuador). On returning to England on a captured Spanish vessel, they rescued Alexander Selkirk (see ROBINSON CRUSOE) from one of the Juan Fernandez Islands (1709). During this journey, Dover had time to concoct a batch of "Dover's powder" with which he cured 172 of his sailors of plague.

DRACONIAN Barbarously severe, harsh, cruel.

Draco Athenian lawgiver who prepared the first code of laws for Athens about 621 B.C. His judgment was severe—he advocated death for all offenses, whether it be stealing an apple from an orchard or murder. Thus, any severely harsh judgments are known today as draconian.

DUN To importune a debtor persistently for payment; a demand for payment.

Joe Dun A famous London bailiff (circa 1820) who was exceedingly efficient in catching defaulting debtors. "You better dun him for the money" was a popular phrase of that time.

DUNCE   A stupid person, dope, numbskull.

John Duns Scotus (1265?–1309)   A Scottish philosopher and theologian. His scholastic philosophy sharply separated philosophy from theology, and argued that God's reason and goodness are an expression of divine will. He also maintained that God could change or suspend the last seven of the Ten Commandments, presumably because there were now new prohibitions which did not exist in Moses' day. The "Dunsmen" or "dunses" represented an important school of Christian theology until they were somewhat discredited by the humanist theologians of the Renaissance. According to the followers of Thomas Aquinas and other critics, a "Duns" or "Dunce" was a philosophical adherent of Duns Scotus, and thereby a hair-splitter who objected for the sake of objecting. Thus, in time, a dunce came to mean someone who was fanatic about details, but had no real capacity for learning.

DUXELLES SAUCE   A purée of mushrooms and onions and seasonings.

Marquis d'Uxelles (circa 17th century)   Employer of the famous chef François Pierre de la Varenne (who wrote "Le Cuisinier François" in 1651) and who no doubt created the sauce.

E

ECHO The repetition of a sound by reflection of sound waves from a surface.

Echo In Greek mythology, a nymph who, because of her unreturned love for Narcissus, pined away until only her voice remained.

EDGAR Statuettes awarded annually by the Mystery Writers of America for the best mystery novel, short story, etc.

Edgar Allan Poe (1809–1849) American poet and famed mystery writer; among his well-known works: *The Fall of the House of Usher, Tales of the Grotesque and Arabesque, Murders in the Rue Morgue, The Mystery of Marie Roget,* and *The Raven* and other poems.

EDWARDIAN Characteristic of the time of Edward VII, especially with reference to literature and art.

Edward VII (1841–1910) Eldest son of Queen Victoria, ruled the British Empire after her death and gave his name to the first decade of the 20th century. Prince of Wales for 60 years, he was a leader of fashionable society.

EGGS BENEDICT Poached eggs served over ham on a split, toasted English muffin covered with hollandaise sauce.

Mr. and Mrs. Legrand Benedict   The couple credited with the idea for the dish. Early in the 20th century at the legendary Delmonico's Restaurant in New York City, Mr. and Mrs. Benedict complained that there was nothing new on the menu. The maître d' asked what she might suggest. Out of their conversation came the now internationally famous recipe, or so the story goes as told by Morris West, editor of *The American Heritage Dictionary*. Actually, the dish was probably invented by Commodore E. C. Benedict (1834–1920), an American banker and yachtsman.

EIFFEL TOWER   Famous Paris landmark.
A. G. Eiffel (1832–1923)   French engineer who designed the tower of iron framework in Paris built for the International Exposition of 1889. It is 948 feet high.

EINSTEINIUM   A radioactive element discovered in the debris of the first thermonuclear explosion.
Albert Einstein (1879–1955)   U.S. physicist born in Germany; formulated theory of relativity.

EISENHOWER JACKET   A short, waist-hugging jacket.
Dwight David Eisenhower (1890–1969)   U.S. general and 34th president of the U.S. (1953–1961).

He popularized this type of jacket when he was commander of Allied forces in Europe during World War II.

ELECTRA COMPLEX Unconscious libidinal feelings for the father, generally manifesting itself first in girls between the ages of three and five.

Electra In Greek mythology, a daughter of Clytemnestra and Agamemnon. With her brother Orestes she avenged the murder of her father by killing her mother and her mother's lover, Aegisthus.

ELYSIAN Blissful, delightful.

Elysium In Greek mythology, the abode of the blessed after death. Also called "Elysian Fields."

ELZEVIR A compact typeface.

Elzevir A family of 17th-century Dutch printers. Louis founded the business at Leiden circa 1580. His five sons all followed in his footsteps, as did his grandsons and great-grandsons. All in all, there were Elzevirs printing in the Netherlands from 1580 to 1712.

EPICURE A person with refined taste in food and wine.

Epicurus (342–270 B.C.) A Greek philosopher who advocated sensuous pleasure as the highest good. He was devoted to the pursuit of pleasure, fond of good food, comfort and ease, and was hedonistic. But he also had a temperate side; he emphasized that prudence, honor, and justice should be coupled with the aforementioned.

ERASTIANISM   A doctrine stressing the submission of the church to civil authority in all matters.

Thomas Erastus (1524–1583)   A German-Swiss theologian, physician and philosopher whose real last name was Lieber. He participated in theological conferences at Heidelberg in 1560 and at Maulbroon in 1564. He wrote many books on excommunication, but wasn't excommunicated himself, which is strange considering the position he took.

ERISTIC   Of or relating to argument, controversy, or discord.

Eris   The Greek goddess of strife and discord.

ESPERANTO   An artificial international language invented in 1887 characterized by a vocabulary based on word roots common to many European languages.

Dr. Esperanto (d. 1917)   The pseudonym of Dr. L. L. Zamenhof, a Polish philologist (someone who loves literature, learning, and study) and oculist who practiced as an oculist in Warsaw. He advocated this international language which he invented in order to promote international understanding and peace. "Esperanto" according to the doctor means "one who hopes." Although there was a great deal of interest in Esperanto into the early 20th century, it never caught on.

EUCLIDEAN   Of, or referring to, the basic works of Euclid.

Euclid   Greek mathematician who published a work in geometry circa 300 B.C. His book *Elements* was the basis for many modern works in geometry.

EUGENIE HAT   Ostrich feather-trimmed hat.

Empress Eugenie (1826–1920)   Empress of the French from 1853–1871. A Spaniard by birth, she was educated in Paris and married Napoleon III soon after he became emperor in December, 1852. She was a leader in fashion and contributed much to the brilliance of the French court. The elegant, lavishly trimmed Eugenie hat is named after her.

EUHEMERISM   The theory that mythology or folklore is based on real persons or events.

Euhemerus (circa 300 B.C.)   Greek mythology expert of the late 4th century B.C.; he wrote *Sacred History*, a philosophical work in which he rationalized the Greek myths, depicting the gods as originally human heroes and warriors, and asserting that the myths were distorted representations of historical events.

EUSTACHIAN TUBE A slender tube between the middle ear and the pharynx.

Bartolommeo Eustachio (1524?–1574) An Italian anatomist considered one of the founders of modern anatomy. He was the first to describe the Eustachian tube in the ear, and also the Eustachian valve of the heart.

F

FAHRENHEIT A temperature scale.

Daniel Gabriel Fahrenheit (1686–1736) A German physicist who lived most of his life in Holland and England. During his time there were many different systems of measuring temperature. Most used water or alcohol in their thermometers. Fahrenheit switched to mercury. His scale depended on certain fixed points. He designated "freezing" as the level in his "tube" when it was put into ice and water. It came to 32 degrees and was labeled the "freezing point." A thermometer was put into the mouth of a healthy man. Fahrenheit designated this point as 96 degrees. In his writings he noted that freezing point temperatures worked better in winter than in summer and he somewhat misguidedly noted that if the thermometer was to be used for sick people, the scale had to be lengthened, as he put it, to 128 or 132 degrees.

FALLOPIAN TUBE Either of two slender tubes that carry ova from the ovaries to the uterus.

Gabriel Fallopius (1523–1562) Italian anatomist, born in Modena, Italy. He discovered the function of the tubes, and described many other anatomical structures as well.

FARAD A unit of quantity of electricity, used especially in electrolysis.

Michael Faraday (1791–1867) A British scientist noted especially for his work in electricity and magnetism.

FATIMID Designating, or of, a dynasty of Moslem rulers.

Fatima (A.D. 606?–632) The daughter of Mohammed. Any of her descendants are called Fatimids.

FAUNA The animals of a specified region or time.

Fauna In Roman mythology, the sister or wife of Faunus. Faunus was a god of nature, the patron of farming and animals, and a good friend of the Greek god Pan. The term was adopted by Linnaeus in 1746 as a term parallel to flora. (See FLORA and PANIC).

FAUSTIAN   Worldly, devilish.

Faust   A magician and alchemist; hero of several dramatic works (notably by Marlowe and Goethe) who sells his soul to the devil in exchange for power and worldly experience. The name is German, after Johann Faust, a real person who was a 16th-century magician and astrologer.

FEDORA   A soft felt hat with a brim that can be turned up or down and a rather low crown creased lengthwise.

Fedora (1881)   The name of a play by Victorien Sardou (1831–1908). The leading character wore a hat fitting the fedora's description and the men in the audience apparently liked it, because they rushed out and had their hatters make it up for them. The play is long forgotten, but those who adopted the hat—not knowing what to call it—gave it the play's name and the Fedora was born.

FERRIS WHEEL   A large upright wheel revolving on a fixed axle and having seats hanging from the frame.

George W. G. Ferris (1859–1896)   Builder of the first Ferris wheel for the World's Fair in Chicago in 1893. He was a U.S. engineer who had worked on railroad and bridge construction.

FINK A hired strikebreaker; one who informs against another.

Pinkerton Pinkerton men were private detectives, often hired as strikebreakers. Known as "Pinks", they were thought to be the original *finks*. (See PRIVATE EYE).

FLAMINIAN WAY A Roman road extending north from Rome to Rimini, built in 220 B.C.

Gaius Flaminius (d. 217 B.C.) Roman statesman and general who built two great public works, the Circus Flaminius, and the Via Flaminia, a military road from Rome to Rimini. Defeated by Hannibal and killed at Lago di Trasimeno in 217, his son Gaius became governor of Hispania Citerior, and also used his soldiers to build a military road from Bologna to Arezzo.

FLETCHERISM The practice of eating small amounts of food by slow and thorough mastication.

Horace Fletcher (1849–1919) Businessman and researcher in the field of human nutrition. He attributed his own health to thorough chewing of his food. He wrote and lectured widely on nutrition, popularizing his ideas until *fletcherism* and *fletcherize* became part of the American language.

FLORA Plants collectively, especially the plants of a certain region.

Flora   In Roman mythology, the goddess of flowers. (See FAUNA).

FORSYTHIA   Any of several shrubs of the genus *Forsythia*, native to Asia.

William Forsythe (1737–1841)   A British botanist and gardener; Forsythe was superintendent of the Royal Gardens at St. James's and Kensington (1784). The genus of shrubs *Forsythia*, which were introduced from China, is named in his honor. William may or may not have personally brought the shrub from China to England, but what attracted the attention of the Houses of Parliament and signaled him for this honor was the plaster he invented which, when applied to a previously diseased tree, stimulated new growth.

FOURIERISM   A system for reorganizing society into small, self-sufficient, cooperative communities.

F. M. Charles Fourier (1771–1837)   French social scientist and reformer; he devoted himself to methods of improving social and economic conditions. He wrote several books advocating cooperative organizations of society into small groups. Brook Farm (1841–1847), founded near West Roxbury, Massachusetts, was a famous example of a Fourieristic experiment. The communes of the 1960s are a later example of the lifestyle he advocated.

FRANC   The basic monetary unit of France.

King of the Franks, Jean le Bon (1350–1364)   The Latin phrase "francorum rex" or "king of the Franks" appeared on the gold coin which Jean le Bon had struck during his reign.

FRANGIPANI   Any of several tropical American shrubs and trees (genus *Plumeria*); a perfume obtained from this flower; a pastry made with ground almonds.

Marquis Frangipani   16th-century Italian nobleman, said to have invented the perfume. Frangipani is the name of an ancient noble Roman family founded by Leo Frangipani circa 1014. (See PLUMERIA).

FRANKFURTER   A smoked sausage of beef or beef and pork made in long, reddish links.

Frankfurt am Main   A river port and industrial center on the Main in Hesse, West Germany, where the frankfurter was first made.

FRAUNHOFER LINES   The dark lines visible in the spectrum of the sun or a star.

Joseph von Fraunhofer (1787–1826)   A Bavarian optician and physicist; he investigated the refractions of various kinds of glass and was the first to observe the dark lines in the solar spectrum. In 1814 he invented various meters by which he measured wavelengths of light.

FREESIA Any of a genus *Freesia* of South African bulbous plants of the iris family, with fragrant, usually white or yellow, funnelshaped flowers.

F. H. T. Freese (d. 1876) A German physician.

FREUDIAN Pertaining to or in accordance with the psychoanalytic theories of Sigmund Freud.

Sigmund Freud (1856–1939) Austrian physician and neurologist, founder of psychoanalysis. (See ADLERIAN).

FRIDAY The sixth day of the week.

Frigga The wife of Odin and goddess of heaven, presiding over marriage and the home, in Norse mythology.

FRISBEE A plastic saucer-shaped disk tossed back and forth in a game.

Mother Frisbie's Cookies Cookies that came in a container that was similarly shaped as today's mass-manufactured "frisbees" and was originally used for the game by Princeton students.

FUCHSIA Any of various chiefly tropical shrubs of the genus *Fuchsia*, widely cultivated for their showy, drooping purplish, reddish, or white flowers; the color *fuchsia*.

Leonhard Fuchs (1501–1566) A professor of medicine in Germany; he was born only a decade after Columbus discovered America. His favorite pastime was to wander in the woods, mountains and plains studying the plants which grew there. He wrote a famous Latin herbal guide illustrated with more than 500 woodcuts. In London, about 1530, he also published a booklet giving medical advice to those sick with the plague.

G

GALAHAD Any man considered to be noble, pure, chivalrous.

Sir Galahad The purest of the knights of King Arthur's round table, who alone succeeded in the quest for the Holy Grail.

GALATEA A durable cotton fabric, often striped, used in making clothing.

Galatea In Greek mythology, an ivory statue of a maiden, brought to life by Aphrodite in answer to the pleas of the sculptor, Pygmalion, who had fallen in love with his creation. The story is retold in modern form in G. B. Shaw's *Pygmalion*.

GALVANIZE   To arouse into awareness or action; to spur, startle.

Luigi Galvani (1737–1798)   Known as the founder of galvanism because of his researches on the twitching of muscles in frogs' legs caused by a current of electricity. He attributed the movements to animal electricity (1791) but Volta later gave the correct explanation.

GANDY DANCER   Slang for a railroad worker.

Gandy Mfg. Co., of Chicago   Manufacturer, now defunct, of tools. The movement of the railroad laborer working with these tools led to the nickname.

GANYMEDE   A young waiter or bar attendant.

Ganymede   In Greek mythology, a Trojan boy of great beauty whom Zeus carried away to be cupbearer to the gods.

GARAND RIFLE   A semi-automatic, rapid-firing .30 caliber rifle, formerly the standard infantry weapon of the U.S. Army.

John C. Garand   A Canadian by birth, he was naturalized as an American citizen in 1920. He first worked as a toolmaker in Rhode Island and New York City, and then at the U.S. Bureau of Standards as an ordnance engineer. The U.S. Army adopted his Garand rifle as the standard shoulder weapon in 1936.

GARDENIA   Any of various shrubs and trees of the genus *Gardenia,* especially *G. jasminoides,* native to China, having glossy evergreen leaves and large, fragrant, usually white flowers.

Alexander Garden (*1730–1791*)   Naturalist who was also a physician. Born in Aberdeen, Scotland, he resided in South Carolina. He deplored living "so far from the learned world" and carried on an extensive correspondence with other eminent botanists of the 18th century, particularly his good friend Linnaeus, known as the father of botany. Alexander had absolutely nothing to do with the discovery of the gardenia plant, but Linnaeus must have thought a great deal of his friendship—or perhaps he just wanted to make him feel less isolated from the world of botany—because when the gardenia was brought back from China, Linnaeus named it after his old friend. Alexander was so delighted that his little granddaughter was named Gardenia after the plant.

GARGANTUAN   Huge, very large, enormous.

Gargantua   A giant king noted for his enormous physical and intellectual appetites, the hero of Rabelais' satire *Gargantua and Pantagruel.*

GARIBALDI   A loose, high-necked blouse.

Giuseppi Garibaldi (1807–1822)   Italian general and nationalist who spearheaded the movement to unify Italy. He and his men, "the red shirts," wore a kind of high-necked garment which quickly became popular with women in the 19th century.

GARRISON FINISH   A racing term in which the winner comes from the back at the last moment.

Edward H. Garrison (1868–1930)   An American jockey who was well known for his knack of winning by such finishes.

GATLING GUN   An early kind of machine gun having a cluster of barrels around an axis, designed to be successively discharged when rotated.

R. J. Gatling (1818–1903)   American inventor from North Carolina; he patented his Gatling gun on November 4, 1862.

GAUSS   A magnetic unit.

Karl F. Gauss (1777–1855)   Director and professor of astronomy at the observatory in Gottingen, Germany. He demonstrated that a circle can be divided into seventeen equal arcs by elementary geometry, published many books on the theory of numbers, made many magnetic and electrical researches, and is considered the founder of the mathematical theory of electricity. He proposed an absolute system of magnetic units, the gauss, which is named after him.

GEIGER COUNTER   An instrument used to detect, measure, and record nuclear emanations.

Hans Geiger (*1882–1945*)   A physicist who devoted his life to radium research. He perfected the instrument which bears his name.

GENTIAN   Any of numerous plants of the genus *Gentiana* characteristically having showy blue flowers.

Gentius, King of Illyria (*2nd century B.C.*)   The king credited with discovering the medicinal value of the gentian plant, as reported by Pliny (A.D. 23–79) writing in his book *Natural History,* a kind of encyclopedia that deals with many subjects, including botany. The extract from the root of the gentian is known as *bitters* and is sometimes given to people to increase the appetite. Also a liqueur or cordial called *gentiane* comes from it.

GEORDIE   A guinea, a defunct British gold coin.

St. George   The patron saint of England. The geordie is a Scottish diminutive for the image of Saint George formerly stamped on the coin. The most famous story about St. George is that he killed a dragon in a fight in order to save a king's daughter. St. George was a real person who died in the year A.D. 303.

GEORGETTE   A sheer, strong, silk or silk-like fabric used for dresses, blouses, or trimming.

Madame Georgette de la Plante   19th-century French dressmaker who registered the trademark for the material, which presumably she created.

GERRYMANDER   To divide a state, county, or city into voting districts to give unfair advantage to one party in elections.

Elbridge Gerry (1744–1814)   An American statesman, member of the Massachusetts Provincial Congress, Continental Congress and a signer of the Declaration of Independence and also the Articles of Confederation. During his second term as governor of Massachusetts (1811) he redistricted the state in a way planned to give Republicans continued control. His move was quickly discovered, disapproved of, and gave rise to the infamous term "gerrymander." Nevertheless, Elbridge became Vice President of the U.S. (1813–1814).

GIBSON   A dry martini garnished with a pickled onion instead of an olive.

Charles Dana Gibson (1867–1944)   The man who ordered a martini from bartender Charles Connolly at the Players in New York City circa 1900. Temporarily out of olives, the bartender substituted an onion. Gibson snorted, but sampled the concoction, and liked it. Soon others would order "that drink you make for Gibson" and the drink was born.

GIBSON GIRL The idealized American girl of the 1890s.

Charles Dana Gibson (1867–1944) American illustrator who created the Gibson girl, who was usually sketched wearing a tailored shirtwaist with leg-of-mutton sleeves, and a long skirt. Gibson's drawings appeared in many magazines of the time, *Life, Scribner's, Century, Harper's,* and his "girl" quickly became the ideal of that era.

GILBERT The centimeter-gram-second electromagnetic unit of magnetomotive force.

William Gilbert (1540–1603) English physician and physicist. His experiments in magnetism and his use for the first time of the terms *electric force, electric attraction,* and *magnetic pole* gained him the title the "father of electricity."

GILSONITE A natural black bitumen found in Utah and Colorado.

S. H. Gilson Discoverer of this material, which is used in the manufacture of acid, alkali, and water-proof coatings. Also called "uintaite."

GIMLET A cocktail of gin or vodka with lime juice.

Sir T. O. Gimlette (1879–1917)   A British naval surgeon (and optimist!) who felt that his gimlet was healthier than drinking straight gin or vodka.

GLADSTONE BAG   A piece of light hand luggage consisting of two hinged compartments.

W. E. Gladstone (1809–1898)   British statesman, four times prime minister, who had his luggage man make such a bag, and often carried it.

GLOXINIA   A cultivated tropical plant of the genneria family with large downy leaves and bell-shaped flowers of various colors.

Benjamin Peter Gloxin   An 18th-century German physician and botanist who discovered the genus *Gloxinia*.

GOETHITE   A hydrous oxide mineral of iron.

Johann Wolfgang von Goethe (1749–1832)   German poet and dramatist; he exercised a dominant influence on the development of German literature. The mineral was named after him in honor of his studies in geology and mineralogy.

GOLCONDA   A source of great riches, as a mine.

Golconda   An ancient city in India near Hyderabad, now in ruins. It was noted for diamond cutting in the 16th century.

GOLGOTHA   A place of burial or a place of agony and sacrifice.

Golgotha   In the Bible, the place where Jesus was crucified (Mark 15:22).

GOLLIWOG   A grotesque person.

Golliwog   Arbitrary formation, after polliwog. A grotesque doll used in illustrations by Florence K. Upton (d. 1922) for a series of children's books.

GONGORISM   A florid, cluttered literary style.

Luis de Gongora y Argote (1561–1627)   Spanish poet who wrote lyrical poems and several dramas in his early years. Later, he affected elegance and euphemism of style known as Gongorism or, in a later exaggerated form, cultism. This poetry was obscure and often meaningless, full of conceits, artificial antitheses, extreme inversions of root meanings, exaggerated metaphors, etc.

GORDIAN KNOT   Any perplexing problem.

King Gordius   In Greek legend, King Gordius of Phrygia tied the knot which an oracle revealed would be undone only by the future master of Asia. Alexander the Great, as legend has it, failed to untie it but cut the knot with his sword.

GORGON   Any ugly or terrifying woman.

Gorgon In Greek mythology, any of three sisters so horrible to see that the beholder was turned to stone.

GRACE
A pleasing quality, favor, thanks; an attractive quality, feature, manner.

The Three Graces In Greek mythology, the three sister goddesses who had control over pleasure, charm, and beauty in human life and in nature. Their names were Aglaia (brilliance), Euphrosyne (joy) and Thalia (bloom). All the derivatives—graceful, graceless, gracious, etc.—also derive from them.

GRADGRIND
Total materialist.

Thomas Gradgrind A materialistic hardware merchant in Charles Dickens' novel *Hard Times*.

GRAHAM CRACKER
A cracker made of finely ground whole wheat flour.

Sylvester Graham (1794–1851) Born in West Suffield, Connecticut; an American advocate of temperance and food reform, especially of the use of the whole of wheat unbolted and coarsely ground in making flour, hence his popular graham cracker and graham flour.

GRAM'S METHOD
A method of staining bacteria for classification.

Hans Christian Joachim Gram (*1853–1938*) A Danish physician; he devised the method which is named after him. It involves the use of Gentian violet, an iodine solution and alcohol. The violet stain is retained by Gram positive bacteria and lost by Gram negative bacteria when the alcohol is applied—an enormous step in aiding science to classify bacteria.

GRANGERIZE To over-illustrate.

James Granger (*1723–1776*) An obscure parson in the village of Shiplake, Oxfordshire, England. He published a book called *A Biographical History of England*. The reader was instructed to illustrate the many-volumed history by collecting engraved portraits and pasting them in the designated places. The idea became very popular with young society ladies. Magnificently illustrated copies of the *Biographical History* still exist (British Museum), one with as many as three thousand portrait engravings. Granger himself was a very popular fellow, although his liberal views caused Dr. Johnson to comment about him: "The dog is a Whig. I do not like to see a Whig in a parson's gown." Later, Granger published one of his sermons on industriousness and dedicated it to "the inhabitants of the parish of Shiplake who neglect the service of the church and spend the Sabbath in the worst kind of idleness." He had delivered the original sermon before the Archbishop of

Canterbury in 1775, who was so impressed he urged its publication.

GRAUSTARKEAN   Colorful, implausible, highly romantic or melodramatic situations or circumstances.

Graustark   An imaginary kingdom in novels by G. B. McCutcheon (1866–1928). He also wrote *Brewster's Millions* (1902) and was co-editor of the Lafayette, Indiana, *Daily Courier*.

GREAT SCOTT!   Exclamation of surprise.

General Winfield Scott (1786–1866)   A man of enormous dignity and military style who was nicknamed "old fuss and feathers." His dignity and demeanor when he stood as a candidate for the U.S. presidency (1852) were such that he earned the nickname "great Scott." It thereafter became a humorous ejaculation for the extraordinary or unusual.

GREENGAGE   A variety of plum having yellowish-green skin and sweet flesh.

Sir William Gage   Introduced the plant to England from France in the early 18th century.

GREGG SHORTHAND   A system of speed writing using quickly made symbols to represent letters, words, phrases.

John Robert Gregg (1864–1898)   An Irishman who explained his system of speed writing in *The Phonetic Handwriting*, published in 1888, the year he immigrated to America and introduced it. He developed his system to simplify an earlier one invented by Sir Isaac Pitman, an Englishman (1813–1898) who called his version "phonography—the writing of sounds." The most famous use of shorthand was by Samuel Pepys, who kept a diary in a system of shorthand he devised himself. After he died, scholars figured out his method and his famous diary was published.

GREGORIAN CALENDAR   A corrected form of the Julian calendar now used in most countries of the world.

GREGORIAN CHANT   Unharmonized and unaccompanied chant used chiefly in the Catholic church.

Pope Gregory I (540–604)   Called "Gregory the Great," this pope came from a patrician family. As pope he restored monastic discipline, enforced celibacy of clergy, and was zealous in propagating Christianity. He exerted great influence in doctrinal matters, introduced changes in the liturgy, arranged the Gregorian chant and the calendar, and rewrote religious works.

GRESHAM'S LAW   The theory that when two or more kinds of money of equal denomination but unequal intrinsic value are in circulation, the one of greater value will tend to be hoarded; popularly, the principle that bad money will drive good money out of circulation.

Sir Thomas Gresham (1519?–1579) English financier who was a member of Queen Elizabeth's first council (1558) and founder of the Royal Exchange and Gresham College in London. He observed and commented on the tendency for coins to behave as explained above.

GRIGNARD'S REAGENT A class of reagents which are used in the synthesis of organic compounds.

Victor Grignard (1871–1934) French chemist who discovered the agent, which is very important in organic synthesis work, and shared (with Paul Sabatier) the 1912 Nobel prize for chemistry.

GRIMES GOLDEN PIPPIN A yellow autumn eating apple.

T. P. Grimes West Virginia fruit grower who developed it about 1790.

GRIMM'S LAW A law showing the kinship between various native English words and the English words borrowed from the Classical or Romance languages.

Jakob Grimm (1785–1863) Librarian to Jerome Bonaparte, King of Westphalia (1808). Eventually he accepted the invitation of Frederick William IV of Prussia to settle in Berlin (1841) where he collaborated with his brother Wilhelm on *Kinder und Hausmarchen* (1812 and 1815), well known in English as *Grimm's Fairy Tales*.

GROG   A liquor; especially rum diluted with water.

Admiral Edward ("Old Grog") Vernon (1684–1757)   British Navy officer called "old grog" by his men because of his habit of walking the deck in all weathers in a grogram cloak. When he introduced into the Navy the practice of serving rum mixed with water as an economy, the concoction was called "grog" and has been called that ever since.

GRUBSTREET   Literary hacks.

Grub Street   Name of a London street where many literary hacks lived.

GRUNDYISM   Given to social disapproval.

Mrs. Grundy   A neighbor repeatedly referred to (but never appearing) in Tom Morton's play *Speed the Plough* (1798) with the question "What will Mrs. Grundy say?"—today grundyism or Mrs. Grundy is the personification of conventional social disapproval, prudishness, narrow-mindedness, etc.

GUARNERIUS   A violin made by a member of the Guarneri family.

Guarneri The Italian family of violin-makers of Cremona (17th–18th century), all fine craftsmen, particularly Guiseppe Antonio (1687?–1745), who is credited with creating the famous violin which bears the family name.

GUINEA A defunct British gold coin worth one pound and one shilling.

Guinea Region on the coast of Africa where the gold for the coins was mined.

GUILLOTINE An instrument for beheading by means of a heavy blade dropped between two uprights.

Joseph Ignace Guillotin (1738–1814) A French doctor who advocated a humane beheading machine, if there could be such a thing, to replace the clumsier method of decapitation then in use—a sword or an axe. The guillotine, which was named after him, was first used in 1791. Dr. Guillotin was to benefit from his campaign to substitute the guillotine for an axe when he died on it during the Reign of Terror. During this period of the French Revolution, an estimated 2500 victims who were considered real or reputed counter-revolutionaries lost their heads, albeit humanely, the good doctor among them. (Note: Joseph Guillotin did not invent the machine; he merely advocated its use.)

GUNTER'S CHAIN   A surveyor's chain 66 feet in length: it consists of 100 links, each 7.92 inches long.

Edmund Gunter (1581–1626)   English mathematician and professor of astronomy at Gresham College, London, who invented the chain plus a line, quadrant, and scale also known by his name.

GUPPY   A small brightly-colored freshwater fish.

R. J. Lechmere Guppy   His contributions to natural history are for the most part forgotten, but his name is more familiar than many a better-known naturalist. Guppy was a clergyman of Trinidad who delighted in ichthyology (the study of fishes). In the mid-nineteenth century he sent to the British Museum a collection of New World fishes. Among them was a new species which was highly prized because it ate mosquito eggs. The British were grateful and named it after him, *Gerardinus guppy*. The fish was later renamed *Poecilia reticulata* or *Lebistes reticulatus*, but it still bears the common name "guppy."

GUTENBERG BIBLE   The first printed Bible.

Johann Gutenberg (1400?–1468)   German inventor of printing from movable type; he brought out the first printed Bible. Archbishop Adolph of Nassau, Elector of Mainz, gave recognition to Gutenberg's works (1465) by presenting him with an income (called a benefice) which allowed him to continue his work. Earlier, Gutenberg had experienced many financial difficulties caused by people who sought to exploit his invention and reap the rewards themselves.

H

HADRIAN'S WALL   A stone wall across northern England from Solway Firth to the Tyne built A.D. 122–128 by Hadrian to protect Roman Britain from Northern tribes.

Hadrian (*A.D. 76–138*)   Emperor of Rome from 117 to 138. During his lifetime he strengthened the monarchical system of Rome, rebuilt and named Hadrianapolis (modern Adrianople), and erected many fine buildings, including his mausoleum (now Castel Sant'Angelo), temples to Venus and Rome, the Aelian bridge, etc.

HALLEY'S COMET   A comet with a period of approximately 76 years, the first for which a return was successfully predicted.

Edmund Halley (*1656–1742*)   British astronomer, mathematician, and inventor who correctly predicted the comet's return.

HAM ACTOR   A very poor and, at the same time, egotistical actor.

Hamish McCullough (1835–1885)   An actor who possibly lent his name to this term, according to *Brewer's Dictionary of Phrase and Fable*. He toured with his troupe in Illinois and was known as "Ham" and his company as "Ham's actors." Another theory is that the term derives from all those actors who aspired to play "Hamlet," some good, some pretty bad.

HAMBLETONIAN   A superior strain of horses bred in the U.S. Also an annual harness race for three-year-old trotters.

Hambletonian   The name of a great stallion (1849–1876) from whom others are descended.

HAMBURGER   Ground beef shaped into a patty and cooked.

Hamburg, Germany   A seaport and state in northwest Germany, on the Elbe River, where hamburgers were first made and which were originally called "Hamburgs," and are often still called "hamburgs" today.

JOHN HANCOCK   One's signature.

John Hancock (1737–1793)   American revolutionary statesman; he graduated from Harvard in 1854 and was elected to the Massachusetts legislature (1766–1772), the Continental Congress, of which he was president (1775–1777), and became the first signer of the Declaration of Independence. His name became synonymous with a signature because his, on the Declaration of Independence, is bold and legible.

HANSARD   One of the official reports of British parliamentary proceedings and debates. Also *hansardize,* chiefly British: to point out or confront with one's previous, inconsistent remarks.

Luke Hansard (1752–1828)   English printer who printed the House of Common's journals from 1774. Official reports of parliamentary proceedings in England are still known as "hansards."

HANSEN'S DISEASE   Leprosy.

A. G. H. Hansen (1841–1912)   Norwegian physician who discovered the germ which causes leprosy in 1879.

HANSOM   A two-wheeled, covered carriage with the driver's seat behind and above.

Joseph Aloysius Hansom (1803–1882)   English architect who designed houses, churches, and various public buildings including the Birmingham, England, town hall in 1833. In 1834 he designed the "safety cab." Safety features included a suspended axle, very large wheels which reached to the roof of the vehicle, and a body close to the ground. It looked like a shiny black box on wheels. Since the driver sat behind, it allowed an unobstructed view in front for the passengers. This feature alone accounted for its immediate popularity.

HAVELOCK A cloth covering for a cap, having a flap to protect the back of the neck.

Henry Havelock (1795–1857) British soldier who distinguished himself during the Sepoy Mutiny (1857), was made a major general in 1857, relieved Lucknow in September, 1857, and held it against a native siege until help arrived in the person of Sir Colin Campbell, November, 1857. Havelock served thirty-four years in India with only a single furlough to England. To protect his head from the fierce heat of the Indian summers he improvised white linen cap covers (resembling those worn in the early Crusades) which were long in the back and protected necks in the sun. These useful articles almost immediately acquired his name and an international reputation. Havelock was such a loyal soldier of the Empire that when a soldier near him succumbed to a bullet, he said: "His was a happy death. He died in the service of his country."

HEBEPHRENIA A form of schizophrenia, characterized by childish or silly behavior and regression to childhood.

113

Hebe The Greek goddess of youth, daughter of Hera and Zeus; she lends her name to this behavior, and also to the word "hebetic," which means youthful.

HECTOR To intimidate or dominate in a blustering way.

Hector A Trojan prince killed by Achilles in Homer's *Iliad*; he was a bully and had the unfortunate habit of *hectoring*.

HEGELIAN A follower of Hegel, or his philosophy.

Georg Wilhelm Friedrich Hegel (1770–1831) German philosopher whose system of thesis, opposing antithesis, and resulting synthesis was the leading system of metaphysics during the second quarter of the 19th century.

HELIOTROPE Any of several plants of the genus *Heliotropium* native to South America, having small, fragrant, purplish flowers. They thrive in the sun.

Helios The Greek sun god, son of Hyperion, depicted as driving his chariot across the sky from east to west daily. Helios also gives his name to the heliostat, an instrument in which a mirror is automatically moved so that it reflects sunlight in a constant direction; heliotaxis, the movement of an organism in response to the light of the sun; heliotherapy, medical therapy involving exposure to sunlight, and many other words.

HEPPLEWHITE Designating a style of furniture characterized by the use of graceful curves.

George Hepplewhite (d. 1786) An English cabinetmaker with offices in the parish of St. Giles, Cripplegate, London, who became famous for the delicacy and beauty of the furniture he designed.

HERCULEAN A task calling for great strength, size or courage; very difficult to do.

Hercules In Greek and Roman mythology, the son of Zeus and Alcmene, renowned for feats of strength, especially twelve prodigious labors imposed on him.

HERMAPHRODITIC Of, or having, the nature of a hermaphrodite.

Hermaphrodite In Greek mythology, a person or animal with the sexual organs of both the male and the female. Also Hermaphroditus, a Greek god, the son of Aphrodite and Hermes, loved by the nymph Salmacis, who wished to unite with him in one body. The union took place and a hermaphrodite developed, an individual with both male and female characteristics. Also, hermaphrodite brig, a two-masted ship.

HERMETIC   Having to do with the occult sciences, especially alchemy, magic; completely sealed.

Hermes Trismegistus   The Greek name for the Egyptian god Thoth, mythological founder of alchemy and other occult sciences. Hermes, usually pictured with winged shoes and hat, carrying a caduceus, was also the god of science, commerce, eloquence, and cunning, and guide of departed souls to Hades. Hermetic, meaning completely sealed by fusion, soldering, etc., derives from the use in alchemy.

HERTZIAN WAVES   Radio waves or other electromagnetic radiation resulting from the oscillations of electricity in a conductor.

H. R. Hertz (1857–1894)   German physician and professor at the University of Bonn. He spent his years investigating Maxwell's electronic theory of light. He demonstrated the existence of electric or electromagnetic waves ("hertzian waves") as early as 1886 and his discoveries led to the development of the wireless telegraph.

HESSIAN BOOTS   High, tasseled men's boots introduced into England in the 19th century by Hessian troops.

Hesse, Germany   A state, 8,150 square miles in area, of central West Germany; the capital is Wiesbaden.

HESSITE   A mineral.

G. H. Hess (1802–1850)   Swiss chemist who discovered this silver telluride, a mineral found in gray masses, which can be cut with a knife.

HINDENBURG   A German dirigible, the largest rigid airship ever built (804 feet long, capable of lifting nearly 473,000 pounds). It was launched at Friedrichshafen, Germany, in 1936 and completed several transatlantic crossings before crashing in flames at Lakehurst, New Jersey, on May 6, 1937, killing 36 of the 97 persons aboard. Apparently, as it was about to anchor to its mast, atmospheric electricity ignited a hydrogen leak and it burst into flames, thus ending travel by rigid airship forever.

Paul von Hindenburg (1847–1934)   German field marshal during World War I and the second president of the Weimar Republic (1925–1934). His presidency was wracked by political unrest, economic depression, and the rise to power of Adolf Hitler, whom he appointed chancellor in 1933.

HIPPOCRATIC OATH   The oath generally taken by students receiving a medical degree; it sets forth an ethical code for the medical profession. (Today, sometimes sardonically referred to as the "hypocritic oath.")

Hippocrates (460?–360? B.C.)   Greek doctor who is called "the father of medicine." Older doctors tried to cure sick people with magic. Hippocrates was the first to study nature instead of magic, and the first to say the sick needed rest, fresh air, light, cleanliness, and proper food. He originated the Oath of Hippocrates to which young doctors swear today. It binds them to honor their teachers, do their best for the sick, never give poisons, and keep the secrets of their patients.

HOBBISM   The philosophy that a strong government is needed to control clashing individual interests.

Thomas Hobbes (1588–1679)   A social philosopher, author of *Leviathan,* he particularly advocated a strong monarchy. He was acquainted with the leading men of his time: Galileo, Gassendi, Mersenne, Ben Jonson, Cowley, Selden. He received a pension from Charles II and spent many years writing books which contained his social philosophy.

HOBSON'S CHOICE   Lack of an alternative.

Thomas Hobson (circa 1690)   Owner of the leading livery stable in the university town of Cambridge, England. He established a firm rule that each customer must take the horse nearest the door when he arrived. He tolerated no exceptions to his rule, so concerned was he about the welfare of his horses. Thus "Hobson's choice" quickly came to mean having no choice at all.

HODGKIN'S DISEASE A usually chronic, sometimes fatal disease, marked by inflammatory enlargement of various organs.

Thomas Hodgkin (1788–1866) English physician who described this form of cancer named after him.

HOLLANDAISE SAUCE A creamy sauce of butter, egg yolks, and lemon or vinegar, used with seafood and vegetables such as asparagus and broccoli.

Holland The country where the sauce originated. Someone traveled there, ate and liked hollandaise sauce, and promptly brought it back to England, where it traveled to America—and everywhere else. Unfortunately, no one knows who or when.

HOMBURG A man's felt hat having a soft, dented crown and a shallow, slightly rolled brim.

Homburg, Germany A town near Wiesbaden, West Germany, where the hats were first manufactured.

HOOLIGAN A hoodlum, especially a young one.

Hooligan or Houlihan The name of an Irish family in Southwark, London (circa 1820), from whom the term "hooligan" is said to have derived.

HOOKER A prostitute.

Joseph Hooker (1814–1879) Union general in the Civil War. It's disputed but often cited that the word "hooker" as a term for a prostitute originated with Hooker's troops' enthusiastic patronage of these ladies-of-the-night during the Civil War. Hooker himself was a graduate of West Point; he retired as a major general in 1868.

HORATIAN   Characteristic of Horace or his poetry.

Horace (65–8 B.C.)   Roman lyric poet and satirist who enjoyed the patronage of Maecenas, the Roman statesman and patron of literature, and received from him the gift of a villa on the Sabine Hill, which Horace celebrated in his verses. He also enjoyed the favor of the Emperor Augustus. (See AUGUST.) Among his works are two books of satires, one book of epodes, four books of odes, two books of epistles, and the *Ars Poetica*. Horace's full name was Quintus Horatius Flaccas.

HOYLE, ACCORDING TO   According to the rules and regulations; in the prescribed, fair way.

Edmond Hoyle (1671–1769)   An English authority on card games and chess who brought out a book of rules and instructions for indoor games, especially card games, which quickly became the standard and authority for all players. "According to Hoyle" soon took on a broader meaning for anything that was done correctly, or playing according to the rules of the game.

HUSSITE   A follower of John Huss.

John Huss (In German, Johannes Hus von Husinetz) *(1360?–1415)*   A Bohemian religious reformer who became a priest in 1401. He attended the Council of Constance (1414) under the protection of King Wenceslaus and Emperor Sigismund. Only one year later, in 1415, he was tried by the council for heresy, condemned, and burned at the stake, July 6, 1415. His death caused great indignation. He was the author of many religious works, especially *De Ecclesia,* "On the Church."

HYACINTH   Any of a genus *Hyacinthus* of plants of the lily family.

Hyacinthus   In Greek mythology, Hyacinthus was a youth loved and accidentally slain by Apollo, who caused to grow from his blood a flower bearing the letters AI AI, a Greek cry of sorrow.

HYGIENE   The science of health and its maintenance.

Hygeia   In Greek mythology, the goddess of health.

HYPNOSIS   A sleeplike condition psychically induced.

Hypnos   In Greek mythology, the god of sleep, identified by the Romans with Somnus. (See SOMNOLENT).

I

IRIS Any of a large genus (*Iris*) of perennial plants of the iris family, with sword-shaped leaves and flowers composed of 3 petals and 3 drooping sepals of widely varying color; also, a rainbow.

Iris In Greek mythology, the goddess of the rainbow: in the *Iliad*, she is the messenger of the gods. She also loans her name to the word *iridescent*: producing a display of lustrous, rainbowlike colors.

ITALIC A kind of type in which the letters do not stand upright, but slope toward the right.

Italy The country of the inventor, Aldus Manutius, who, in about the year 1500, dedicated the type to Italy. It was first used in an Italian edition of Virgil printed in 1501.

J

JACK-A-NAPES A conceited, insolent, presumptuous fellow.

Jac Napes The nickname of William de la Pole. This Englishman (1396–1460) was the 4th Earl and

1st Duke of Suffolk. He served fourteen years in the French wars, first under Henry V, then under the duke of Bedford. He was taken prisoner by Joan of Arc in 1429. When freed, he occupied himself with home politics, but he soon fell on hard times. After the renewal of the war with France he was accused by the House of Commons of maladministration partly because he had been responsible for ceding part of the kingdom to France. He was eventually beheaded.

JACK KETCH   An official hangman; chiefly a British expression.

   Jack Ketch   A famous English public executioner circa 1686.

JACOB'S LADDER   (Nautical) A rope or chain ladder with rigid rungs.

   Jacob   The Biblical patriarch who saw the ladder in a dream (Genesis 28:12). There is also a blue flower by this name.

JACQUARD   A loom; the distinctive weave made by that loom.

   J. M. Jacquard (1751–1834)   French inventor of the Jacquard apparatus used in the Jacquard loom for figured weaving; inventor also of a machine for weaving nets.

JACQUERIE A peasant revolt.

Jacques Bonhomme In slang, a French peasant; the archetypal *Jacquerie* was the French peasants' revolt of 1358.

JANSENISM The theological principles which emphasize predestination, deny free will, and maintain that human nature is incapable of good.

Cornelis Jansen (1585–1638) A professor, bishop of Ypres, and author who was condemned as a heretic by the church; he maintained that the teaching of St. Augustine on grace, free will, and predestination was opposed to the teaching of the Jesuit schools. In the religious controversies he provoked, his view was championed by Pascal, Arnauld, Nicole and the Port-royalists.

JANUARY The first month of the year.

Janus An ancient Roman god of gates and doorways, depicted with two faces looking in opposite directions, whose festival month was January.

JEFFREY PINE A pine native to Oregon and California.

John Jeffrey 19th-century Scottish botanist who identified the tree.

JEKYLL AND HYDE A two-faced person.

Dr. Jekyll and Mr. Hyde Names of the dual per-
sonalities portrayed in R. L. Stevenson's story *The
Strange Case of Dr. Jekyll and Mr. Hyde*. The good
doctor discovers drugs that enable him to transform
himself into a vicious, brutal creature named Mr.
Hyde and back again.

JEREMIAD A lamentation, tale of woe.

Jeremiah A Hebrew prophet of the 7th and 6th
centuries B.C. The lamentations of Jeremiah are
contained in the Bible.

JEROBOAM A large wine bottle, especially for
champagne, usually holding almost a gallon.

Jeroboam The first of the Kings of Israel (912
B.C.?). He is described in the Bible as "A mighty man
of valor who did sin and make Israel to sin" (I Kings
14:16). This may be the reason the oversized wine
bottle was named for him at the beginning of the
19th century.

JEZEBEL A wicked woman.

Jezebel In the Bible, the wicked woman who
married Ahab, King of Israel. (I Kings 21:5–23:11).

JOHN BULL A personification of England or the
English.

John Bull   A character in *Law is a Bottomless Pit*, a satire by John Arbuthnot (1667–1735), a Scottish writer.

JOHNSON GRASS   A coarse grass cultivated for forage but also often a troublesome weed.

William Johnson   A 19th-century American agriculturist; he developed Johnson Grass and sold it to neighboring farmers for feed.

JOHNSON NOISE   Thermal background noise in a radio receiver.

B. Johnson   A 20th-century U.S. physicist who discovered and identified it.

JOHNSONESE   Characteristic of the literary style of Samuel Johnson.

Samuel Johnson (1709–1784)   English lexicographer, critic, and conversationalist; his literary style is considered to be filled with Latinisms, erudite, heavy, and pompous.

JONAH   Any person said to bring bad luck by being present.

Jonah   In the Bible, a Hebrew prophet thrown overboard in a storm sent because he had disobeyed God. He was swallowed up by a big fish but three days later was cast up on the shore unharmed.

JOSEPH'S COAT   A tropical plant cultivated for variously colored foliage.

Joseph   In the Bible, the 11th son of Jacob (Genesis 30:22–24). He was sold into slavery by his jealous brothers after he received a beautiful multicolored coat from his father.

JOSHUA TREE   A treelike plant of the southwestern part of the U.S.

Joshua   Prophet who gives his name to the tree because the extended branches emulate the outstretched arms of Joshua as he pointed with his spear to the city of Ai (Joshua 89:18).

JOVIAL   Marked by hearty conviviality.

Jove   Another name for Jupiter, the supreme god, patron of the Roman state, brother and husband of Juno, akin to the Greek god Zeus.

JOVIAN   Of or like Jove, the god Jupiter; majestic.

Jupiter   In Roman mythology, the god ruling over all the other gods and all people. (See JUNO.)

JUDAS   A traitor, betrayer.

Judas Iscariot   The disciple who betrayed Jesus (Matthew 26:14, 48).

127

JULIAN CALENDAR Introduced in 46 B.C., in which the ordinary year had 365 days and every fourth year, leap year, had 366 days. The months were the same as in the Gregorian or New Style calendar now used.

JULY The seventh month of the year.

Julius Caesar (100–44 B.C.) Famous Roman statesman and general who introduced the calendar in 46 B.C. He was prevented by death from completing other reforms he planned, including codifying the law, draining the Pontine marshes, enlarging the harbor at Ostia, and building a canal through the Isthmus of Corinth.

JUNOESQUE Stately and regal. **JUNE** The sixth month of the year.

Juno In Roman mythology, the sister and wife of Jupiter; queen of the gods, and goddess of marriage.

K

KAFKAESQUE Surreal, nightmarish, bafflingly complex.

Franz Kafka (1883–1924) Austrian poet and writer of psychological and philosophical fiction; he was born in Prague of Jewish parentage. His works include the posthumously published novels *The Trial* (1925), *The Castle* (1926), and *Amerika* (1927).

KAHN TEST   A modified form of the Wassermann test for diagnosing syphilis. (See WASSERMANN.)

R. L. Kahn (b. 1887)   U.S. immunologist who developed the test.

KAISER ROLL   A large, round, crusty roll, used for sandwiches.

Kaiser   A title (derived from the word *Caesar*) designating the emperors of the Holy Roman Empire, and Germany. The Kaiser roll was originally made for one of the Kaisers, but no one knows which one!

KANTIAN   A follower of the philosophy of Kant.

Immanuel Kant (1724–1804)   A German philosopher who held that the content of knowledge comes from the senses but that its form is determined by the mind.

KENNY METHOD (or TREATMENT)   An earlier method for treating polio.

Elizabeth Kenny (1886–1952)   Australian nurse who became famous for her method of treating the disease, which consisted of hot packs and exercises.

KEWPIE DOLL A trademark for a chubby, rosy-faced doll with a topknot, patterned after a drawing by Rose O'Neil.

Cupid The god of love, son of Venus, usually represented as a winged boy with a bow and arrow. "Kewpie" was simply an altered form of "Cupid."

KEYNESIAN A supporter of John Maynard Keynes' economic theories.

John Maynard Keynes, First Baron Keynes (1883–1946) A British economist who was the principal representative of the Treasury at the Paris Peace Conference in 1919, editor of the *Economic Journal* from 1912, and the author of many books on monetary reform and economics.

KREBS CYCLE A series of biochemical reactions which produce carbon dioxide.

H. A. Krebs (1900–1951) British biochemist who identified the cycle.

L

LACONIC Brief or terse in speech or expression; using few words.

Laconia   The ancient region of the Peloponnesus of which Sparta was the metropolis. The Laconians were known for their brevity of speech. When Philip of Macedon threatened to invade their land (see PHILIPPIC) he sent this message: "If I enter Laconia, I will level Sparta [the capital city] to the ground." The Laconians replied laconically with one word: "If."

LADY BOUNTIFUL   A charitable woman.

Lady Bountiful   A character in Farquhar's comedy *The Beaux' Strategem* in 1707. Her name now stands for a charitable woman, especially one who gives ostentatiously, as she did.

LAFFER CURVE   A theory which maintains that increasing tax rates cause a reduction in revenues by discouraging production and investment.

A. Laffer (b. 1940)   U.S. economist who formulated the graph which illustrates this theory.

LAMAZE METHOD   A method of natural childbirth emphasizing breathing control and relaxation and the role of the father to help bring these about.

F. Lamaze   20th-century French physician who developed the technique.

LANGLEY   A unit of illumination used to measure the temperature of a star.

Samuel Langley (1834–1906) An American astronomer, inventor and aeronautical pioneer. With only a high school education, he excelled in many disciplines. He began to study the possibilities of flight at an early age and built models of planes. His model no. 5 achieved a flight of 3000 ft. on the Potomac River on May 6, 1896—years before the Wright brothers. A full-sized machine, designed to carry a pilot, failed in two trials on October 8 and December 8, 1903 (a year before the Wright brothers flew). However, Langley lacked the funds for further experiments, so the Wright brothers got the credit for flying. Langley Field, the flying field near Norfolk, Virginia, is named in his honor and his machine is on exhibition in the National Museum, Washington, D.C.

LARES AND PENATES The treasured belongings of a family or household.

Lares and Penates Originally gods of cultivated fields worshipped by each household at the crossroads where its allotment of land joined others. Later, the lares (singular: lar) were worshipped in the houses in association with the Penates (the gods of the storeroom) (singular: penus) and thus of the family's prosperity. Each household had a lar which was represented as a youthful figure dressed in a short tunic holding in one hand a drinking horn, in the other a cup. A prayer was said to the lar every morning and special offerings were made at festivals.

LAVALIERE or LAVALIER An ornament hanging from a chain worn about the neck.

Duchesse de la Vallière, Françoise Louise de la Baume Le Blanc (1644–1710) A mistress of Louis XIV (1661–1674) and mother of four of his children. She was superseded by Marquise de Montespan and retired to a convent in 1674. She favored lavalieres and made them popular at court.

LAVOISIA A showy Brazilian shrub.

Antoine Laurent Lavoisier (1743–1794) Known as the founder of modern chemistry; he made important contributions in his field. But he also had an interest in botany, and it was this interest that led his botanist friends to name the Lavoisia after him. Lavoisier was convicted of anti-revolutionary activities during the French Revolution and guillotined.

LAWRENCIUM A synthetic element.

Ernest O. Lawrence (1901–1958) An American scientist who was awarded the 1939 Nobel prize in physics for discovering this element. He also invented the cyclotron in 1931, researched the structure of the atom, and produced artificial radioactivity.

LAZAR An impoverished, diseased beggar.

Lazarus The diseased beggar in Jesus' parable of the rich man and the beggar (Luke 16:19–31).

LEOTARD A snugly fitting garment usually made of elastic, originally worn by dancers or acrobats.

Jules Leotard A 19th-century trapeze artist featured in Paris at the *Cirque Napoleon* and in London at the *Club Alhambra*. He was the first to perfect the aerial somersault. Later in his life he published his memoirs which ended with this advice to men: "Do you want to be adored by the ladies? A trapeze is not required, but instead of draping yourself in unflattering clothes, invented by ladies and which give us the air of ridiculous manikins, put on a more natural garb, which does not hide your best features." Of course the garb he advocated was the one he had designed—the leotard.

LESBIAN A homosexual woman. Also, **LESBIANISM** The practice of homosexuality among women.

Lesbos, the Island of A Greek island in the Aegean, off the coast of Asia Minor, where Sappho and her followers extolled the pleasures of lesbianism, circa 7th century B.C. (See SAPPHIC.)

LETHARGY Sluggish indifference, abnormal drowsiness or torpor.

Lethe In Greek mythology, the river of forgetfulness in Hades.

LEVI'S A trademark for closefitting trousers made of denim, reinforced at the seams with small copper rivets.

Levi Strauss   Manufacturer who first made them in San Francisco circa 1850.

LILLIPUTIAN   Very small, tiny.

Lilliput   In Swift's *Gulliver's Travels,* a land inhabited by people about six inches tall.

LIMERICK   A five-line nonsense rhyme, often bawdy, popularized by Edward Lear.

Limerick, Ireland   A county in southwest Ireland in Munster province whose connection with "limericks" is tenuous, despite the fact that the rhyme undoubtedly derives its name from the county. A typical limerick is: There once was a man from Nantucket/Who kept all his cash in a bucket;/But his daughter named Nan/Ran away with a man,/And as for the bucket, Nantucket.

LIMOUSINE   Originally a kind of flowing mantle or coat; also, a luxurious automobile.

Limousin   A region and former province of west-central France. The inventor of this type of car, Charles Jeantaud, was from Limoges in the province of Limousin. An automobile designer and manufacturer, in 1898 he won the world's land speed record with an electric car called the Jeantaud, which traveled at a speed of 39.24 miles per hour.

LINDY HOP   A lively dance for couples, popular in the 1930s.

  Charles A. "Lindy" Lindbergh (1902–1974)   U.S. aviator who made the first nonstop flight ("hop") from New York to Paris in 1927.

LISTERINE   A trademark for an antiseptic mouth-wash.

  Joseph Lister, 1st Baron of Lyme Regis (1827–1912)   A surgeon who made a special study of inflammation and suppuration following injuries and wounds. Deeply influenced by the discoveries of Louis Pasteur, he is considered the founder of antiseptic surgery. He was very unhappy about the use of his name in the mouthwash product but little could be done about it.

LOBELIA   Any of numerous plants of the genus *Lobelia* having terminal clusters of variously colored flowers.

  Mattias de l'Obel or Lobel (1538–1616)   Flemish botanist from Lille who was so skilled with herbs that he eventually was appointed to the English court of James I as the king's physician. It isn't actually known what L'Obel *did* to gain the honor, but lobelia is named after him.

LOBSTER NEWBURG   Shelled lobster in a rich cream and sherry sauce.

Charles Wenberg A 19th-century shipping magnate; he discovered this dish in South America. When he enthused about his discovery to the great restaurauteur Lorenzo Delmonico in New York City it promptly went on the menu as "Lobster Wenberg." Then the two quarreled and Delmonico reversed the first three letters of Wenberg's name, changing the dish to "Newburg," and "Newburg" it remained.

LOGANBERRY A trailing prickly plant, *Rubus loganobaccus,* cultivated for its edible fruit.

*James H. Logan (**1841–1928**)* Teacher in Independence, Missouri, in the 1850s, who then went westward as the driver of an ox team for the Overland Telegraph Company. On reaching California he settled down to study law, eventually serving ten years as the district attorney for Santa Cruz, and twelve as a superior court judge. Logan was also a horticulturist. In 1880 he planted a fruit and vegetable garden. He planted a row of wild California blackberries between a row of raspberries. The next generation seeds were planted and yielded a new kind of blackberry. It proved to have a distinct taste of its own and was named loganberry.

LOGANIA Designating a family *Loganiaceae* of chiefly tropical or subtropical, often poisonous plants.

James Logan (1674–1751)   Secretary to William Penn, mayor of Philadelphia (1722) and Chief Justice, Pennsylvania Supreme Court (1731–1739). When he died he bequeathed his library to Philadelphia, where as the Loganian Library, it is part of the city collection. He was very interested in botany, and a great friend of the botanist John Bartrand. The genus *Logania* was so named by Linnaeus in his honor.

LOMBROSIAN   Designating or of the theories of Lombroso.

Cesare Lombroso (1836–1909)   An Italian physician and criminologist, and professor of psychiatry at Pava (1862). He believed that a criminal represents a distinct anthropological type with definite physical and mental stigmata. According to Lombroso, a criminal is the product of heredity, atavism, and degeneracy.

LOTHARIO   A seducer of women.

Lothario   The name of a young rake in Nicholas Rowe's play *The Fair Penitent* (1703).

LOU GEHRIG'S DISEASE   Amyotrophic lateral sclerosis.

Lou Gehrig (1903–1941)   Much-beloved U.S. baseball player who died of the disease. He was first baseman for the N.Y. Yankees from 1925–1939. He established a batting average for his baseball career of .341 and a record of playing in 2130 consecutive major league games. He retired from baseball in 1939 and was appointed parole commissioner for New York City January 2, 1940.

LOUIS D'OR   A gold coin of France from 1640 to the Revolution; a 20-franc gold coin of post-Revolutionary France, also called "louis."

Louis XIII **(1601–1643)**   He was king of France (1610–1643) when the coin was first minted, and was followed by three more monarchs (Louis XIV, Louis XV, Louis XVI).

LOUIS QUINZE   A style of furniture.

Louis XV   French monarch called the "well-beloved"; he engaged in the Seven Years' War from 1756–1763 which by the Treaty of Paris brought disaster in the loss of Canada and India. He had several mistresses, especially Mme. de Pompadour (see POMPADOUR) whose influence was long-continued and most harmful. Louis Quinze furniture is characterized by rococo treatment with emphasis on curved lines and highly decorative forms based on shells, flowers, etc. Also Louis Quatorze, pertaining to the style of architecture, furniture and decoration of the reign of Louis XIV; Louis Seize, ditto the reign of Louis XVI; Louis Treize, the reign of Louis XIII.

LUCIFER   A friction match.

Lucifer   The archangel cast from heaven for leading a revolt of the angels; Satan.

LUCULLAN   Lavish, luxurious.

Lucius Lucinius Lucullus (110?–57? B.C.)   A Roman general; he was a patron of the arts and literature, and an epicure. He lived in great luxury and established a reputation for the splendor of his banquets and the magnificence of his surroundings. He enjoyed the company of the leading poets, artists, and philosophers of his day.

LUCY STONER   One who advocates that married women use only their maiden names.

Lucy Stone (Mrs. Henry Brown Blackwell) (1818–1893)   A famous American woman suffragist who was married but continued to use her maiden name as an indication that she had not lost her individuality by her marriage. She lectured on women's rights and against slavery, aided in forming the American Woman Suffrage Association in 1869 and raised money for funding *Woman's Journal* in 1870. She was coeditor with her husband from 1872–1893.

LUDDITES   A group of disgruntled workers in England (1811–1816) who smashed new labor-saving textile machinery in a protest against unemployment and reduced wages.

Ned Lud A Leicestershire workman who, in about 1779, broke up stocking frames. Thus the men who copied his behavior a few years later became known as "luddites."

LYNCH Execution without lawful trial, as by hanging.

Captain William Lynch (1741–1820) A Virginia farmer who organized bands to punish outlaws and collaborators with the British during the Revolutionary period. Lynching, of course, was a circumvention of due legal process. The Ku Klux Klan was a large offender, but Captain Lynch was its first and greatest proponent and thereby gave this form of punishment its name.

M

MACADAM Small broken stones combined with a binder such as tar or asphalt used in paving roads, popularly called tarmac.

John L. McAdam (1756–1836) A Scottish engineer who invented the process. He was Surveyor General of roads in Bristol, England, in 1815 and he was upset at the condition of the roads he surveyed. He determined to do something about it, so he devised the process known as "macadamizing" roads, which made quite a difference.

MACADAMIA NUT A spherical, hard-shelled edible nut from an Australian tree, cultivated in Hawaii, etc.

John Macadam (d. 1865) A Scottish chemist in Australia, who was the first to discover and enjoy the Macadamia nut. He was no relation to John L. McAdam, who macadamized roads.

MACH NUMBER The ratio of the speed of an object to the speed of sound in the medium through which the object is moving. For instance, an aircraft moving twice as fast as sound is said to be traveling at Mach 2.

Ernst Mach (1838–1916) Austrian physicist and philosopher who investigated in his researches in physics the physiology and psychology of the senses, especially in relation to the theory of knowledge. He was an early founder of a realistic philosophy based on the analysis of sensations.

MACHIAVELLIAN Crafty and duplicitous.

Niccolò Machiavelli (1469–1527) Florentine statesman and writer on government. He is best known for teaching that the head of a government must be ruthless and expedient. He wrote two great books, *The Prince* and *Discourses*. *The Prince* was dedicated to Lorenzo de Medici, and it was written to teach him how to become an all-powerful ruler and unite Italy. According to Machiavelli, the Prince must do whatever he has to do to be an all-powerful ruler. If it is helpful to lie, steal, and cheat, then so be it. Results are what count.

MACKINAW A short, double-breasted coat of heavy woolen material, usually plaid.

Mackinac An island in Michigan on the Lake Huron side of the Straits of Mackinac where the cloth and the coat were trading items during the 19th century.

MACKINTOSH A raincoat of rubberized cloth, informally called a *mac.*

Charles Mackintosh (1766–1843) A Scottish chemist and inventor who found it particularly distasteful to get his clothing soaked when he went out in inclement weather. After many trials and failures he patented, in 1823, a waterproof fabric, known as mackintosh. Soon after all raincoats were called by this name.

MADEIRA A fortified white to amber wine.

Madeira A group of Portuguese islands in the Atlantic, off the west coast of Morocco, where the wine is made.

MADELEINE A small rich cake baked in a shell-shaped mold.

Madeleine Paulnier A pastry cook who was the Mrs. Fields of the 19th century. Madeleine's concoctions were present at every luncheon, every dinner, every gala. Dessert was not complete without madeleines being served, and they are still popular today.

MAE WEST An inflated life preserver vest for use by aviators downed at sea.

Mae West (1892–1980) Shapely actress who appeared in many early motion pictures with W. C. Fields, and whose large mammary glands resembled, well, an inflated life preserver vest! Mae is forever identified with the slightly risqué, including her famous line "Come up and see me sometime."

MAGINOT LINE A system of heavy fortification built before World War II on the eastern frontier of France. It failed to prevent the invasion by the Nazi armies.

André Maginot (1877–1932) French politician, member of Chamber of Deputies from 1910. He served in World War I, and was minister of colonies (1917), of pensions (1921), and of war (1922–1924). He was a vigorous advocate of military preparedness, so the Maginot line was named in his honor.

MAGNOLIA   Any of various evergreen or deciduous trees and shrubs of the genus *Magnolia* of the Western Hemisphere and Asia, many of which are grown for their showy white, pink, purple, or yellow flowers.

Pierre Magnol (1638–1715)   A contemporary of Michael Bégon (see BEGONIA), he was a French physician and botanist who originated the classification of plants by families. He practiced "physic" in Montpellier for most of his life. That part of France was famous for the variety of its flora, and Magnol began categorizing the local plant life in a book which attracted the attention of botanists from all over the country; they came to study with him at Montpellier. During his lifetime he published a systematic classification of all flora which was later much admired by the famous botanist Linnaeus. Since he discovered the magnolia and brought it to the attention of the populace, it was named for him.

MAHONIA   Any of a genus *Mahonia* of low evergreen shrubs of the barberry family, with clusters of yellow flowers followed by blue berries.

Bernard McMahon (circa 1775–1816)   U.S. botanist who first discovered the plant.

MALAPROPISM   Ludicrous misuse of words, especially through confusion caused by resemblance in sound, for example *progeny* for *prodigy*.

145

Mrs. Malaprop A character in Sheridan's 18th-century play *The Rivals* who makes such blunders in her use of words.

MAN FRIDAY An efficient helper and faithful follower.

Friday The devoted native servant of Robinson Crusoe in Daniel Defoe's novel *Robinson Crusoe*. (See ROBINSON CRUSOE.)

MANN ACT An act of Congress (June, 1910) prohibiting the interstate transportation of women for immoral purposes, as white slavery, prostitution, etc.

James Robert Mann (1856–1922) U.S. congressman who sponsored the legislation that bears his name.

MANSARD ROOF A roof with two slopes on each of the four sides, the lower steeper than the upper.

François Mansard (1598–1666) A French architect. His works include the churches of Sainte-Marie de Chaillot and Visitation de Sainte-Marie, the Hôtel de la Vrillière in Paris, and several chateaux. He created the mansard roof and brought it into general use.

MARATHON A long-distance race.

Marathon, Greece   The site of a victory of Greeks over Persians in 490 B.C., the news of which was carried to Athens by a long-distance runner—and thus the "marathon" was born.

MARCH   The third month of the year.

Mars   The Roman god of war, akin to the Greek god Ares.

MARTENSITE   The chief constituent of hardened carbon tool steels.

Adolf Marten (d. 1914)   A German metallurgist who discovered this substance, which is composed of up to one percent of carbon and a solid solution of iron.

MARTINET   Any strict disciplinarian or stickler for rigid rules.

General Jean Martinet   A 17th-century army officer who served under Louis XIV; he devised a new and rigid system of military drill which was so severe any advocate of strict discipline forever after has been known as a *martinet*.

MARTINI   An alcoholic drink made of gin and vermouth, sometimes vodka and vermouth.

Martini & Rossi   Manufacturers of vermouth; they say that the name originated with them. The drink first made its appearance about 1890, and according to barmen's books of the time it was made of one part gin and two parts sweet vermouth. Today, as any martini drinker knows, the vermouth is a negligible part of the concoction. Some people use an eyedropper to add just a few drops.

MARXISM The system of thought developed by Karl Marx.

Karl Marx (1818–1883) German revolutionary leader, social philosopher and political economist, and the founder of modern socialism.

MASOCHISM The getting of pleasure from suffering.

Leopold von Sacher-Masoch (1835–1895) Austrian author whose popular novels depicted the attainment of sexual pleasure from being dominated, mistreated, or hurt physically by one's partner, and the attainment of pleasure from suffering physical or psychological pain inflicted by others or by oneself. The idea was so contrary to most people's ideas of pleasure that his name quickly came to mean this type of perversion.

MASON JAR A glass jar having a wide mouth and a screw top, used for preserving foods, especially in home canning.

John L. Mason   American who patented his revolutionary Mason jar in 1858. Little is known about him except that he earned the gratitude of thousands of home canners.

MASON-DIXON LINE   A boundary line between Pennsylvania and Maryland regarded, before the Civil War, as separating the free states from the slave states, and now, the North from the South.

Charles Mason and Jeremiah Dixon   Two ordinary working men who surveyed the line in 1763–1767.

MASONITE   A trademark for a kind of hardboard made from pressed wood fiber, used as a building material.

W. H. Mason (1877–1947)   U.S. engineer who invented it.

MAUDLIN   Foolishly and tearfully or weakly sentimental.

Mary Magdalene   Repentant sinner who fell at the feet of Jesus and wept. Magdalene is used as a general name for a repentant woman sinner. Since she is pictured as weeping, the English corruption of her name, maudlin, has taken this meaning.

MAUSOLEUM   A stately tomb or a building housing such a tomb or tombs.

King Mausolos (d. 353 B.C.) King of Caria, an ancient region in southwest Asia Minor. In the 4th century B.C., his wife, Artemisia, built him a magnificent tomb at Halicarnassus—thus all elaborate tombs since have taken his name. It crumbled in an earthquake in 1375, having stood almost 1800 years.

MAVERICK A person who takes an independent stand.

Samuel Augustus Maverick (1803–1870) The Mayor of San Antonio, Texas, in 1839, a member of the Texas Congress in 1845, and a member of the first legislature of the State of Texas. He owned a large (385,000 acres) ranch in the state but contrary to the local customs he refused to have his cattle branded. The term *maverick*, meaning an unbranded animal, arose from this practice. Later, *maverick* came to mean a person who takes an independent stand.

MAXWELL A unit of magnetic flux.

James Maxwell (1831–1879) Scottish physicist who demonstrated that electromagnetic action travels through space in transverse waves similar to those of light and having the same velocity. He advanced the theory that light and electricity are the same in their ultimate nature.

MAY The fifth month of the year.

Maia   In Roman mythology, a goddess of spring, the daughter of Faunus and wife of Vulcan.

MAYONNAISE   A dressing made of beaten egg yolk, butter or olive oil, lemon juice or vinegar, and seasonings.

Mahón, Minorca   City whose capture in 1756 by the Duke of Richelieu is commemorated in the name of this sauce. This French soldier and diplomat was a descendant of Cardinal Richelieu. Presumably he celebrated his military triumph in other ways, as well, but his most lasting memorial to the battle of Mahón is in Mahon-naise.

McGUFFEY READER   A famous school book in the early 1800s.

William Holmes McGuffey (1800–1873)   American educator and professor at the University of Virginia from 1845–1873. He is best known for his series of *Eclectic Readers*. The first and second readers were published in 1836, and were quickly followed by third and fourth readers in 1837. He taught countless youngsters how to read. More than 120,000,000 copies of McGuffey's *Readers* in the original and revised editions have been sold.

McINTOSH   A red eating apple.

John McIntosh An Ontario farmer who found the red apple in 1796 while clearing woodland in Dunclas County. He liked it so much he decided to cultivate it.

MEANDER To follow a winding and turning course.

Maeander A river in southwest Asia Minor, flowing west into the Aegean, with a particularly winding and twisting course. It is now called the Menderes River.

MECHLIN A delicate lace.

Mechlin A city in Belgium noted for its lace.

MÉDOC A red Bordeaux wine.

Médoc, France District in the Bordeaux region of France where this wine was originally made.

MEDUSA A repulsively ugly or terrifying woman.

Medusa In Greek mythology, a woman who had snakes for hair and eyes which, if looked into, turned the beholder into stone.

MELBA TOAST Stale bread sliced thin and toasted until brown and crisp.

Nellie Melba (1861–1931) Opera singer whose real name was Helen Porter Mitchell. She was born near Melbourne, Australia, and took her stage name from this city. She made her operatic debut at Brussels in 1887 and her London debut in 1888. She quickly became, well, the "toast" of the town. She toured the United States, became prima donna at the Royal Opera, Covent Garden, London, and in 1918 was created Dame of the British Empire by the King.

MENDEL'S LAWS The four principles of hereditary phenomena discovered and formulated by Gregor Mendel.

Gregor Mendel (1822–1884) An Austrian botanist who entered the order of Augustinians at Brunn in 1843, becoming an abbot. He was known for his breeding experiments with peas in the monastery garden. One thing led to another and he eventually discovered Mendel's laws, laws observed in inheritance of many characteristics in animals and plants. The laws were published by the natural history society of Britain in 1865, but not widely recognized until brought into prominence by Hugo De Vries, a Dutch botanist, and others in 1900.

MENNONITE Any member of an evangelical Protestant Christian sect founded in Friesland in the 16th century and still existing in America and Europe.

153

Menno Simons (1467?–1561?) A Roman Catholic priest who came under the influence of Lutheran and Anabaptist thought and withdrew from the church, was rebaptized, and ordained an elder at Groningen. He was active as the organizer and leader of Anabaptist groups in East Friesland, Holland, and Germany, called Mennonites. Mennonites oppose the taking of oaths, infant baptism, military service, and the acceptance of public office, and favor plain dress and plain living.

MENTOR A wise, loyal adviser.

Mentor In Greek mythology, the loyal friend and adviser of Odysseus and the teacher of his son, Telemachus.

MERCERIZE To treat cotton thread with sodium hydroxide so as to shrink the fiber and increase its color absorption and luster.

John Mercer (1791–1866) An English calico printer and chemist who started working at the age of nine as a bobbin winder. When he was ten, a fellow worker in the textile factory taught him to read and write. He taught himself the art of dyeing. By assiduously studying a chemistry book, he experimented with the reaction of caustic soda, sulfuric acid, and zinc chloride on cotton cloth and paper. The process he invented became known as mercerizing—strengthening the individual cotton fibers by bathing them in a solution of these agents. Cloth so treated absorbed dye much more rapidly. The importance of this discovery greatly enhanced England's fabric industry and led to Mercer's election to the Royal Society.

MERCURIAL Having qualities suggested by Mercury—quick, quick-witted, volatile, changeable, fickle.

Mercury In Roman mythology, he was the messenger of the gods, god of commerce, manual skill, eloquence, cleverness, travel, and thievery. It's easy to see that the alchemists named the element mercury because of its fluidity, its quicksilver quality.

MESMERIZE To spellbind, to hypnotize.

Franz Mesmer (1743–1815) An Austrian physician who believed that some type of occult force existed in him. He made many experiments on the supposed curative powers of the magnet and developed the theory of animal magnetism. In Paris in 1778 he devoted himself to curing diseases; his seances were investigated by a commission of physicians and scientists appointed by the French government. They promptly denounced him as an impostor; however, no one remembers the names of the people who investigated him, while Franz Mesmer's name is world-famous.

MICAWBER An incurable optimist.

Wilkins Micawber A character in Charles Dickens' novel *David Copperfield* who remains doggedly optimistic about a change in luck despite his improvidence and constant adversity. He is always in expectation of "something turning up."

MICHELSON-MORLEY EXPERIMENT An experiment performed in 1887 in an attempt to detect the motion of the earth through the ether by measuring the difference in velocity of two perpendicular beams of light.

Abram Michelson (1852–1931) and Edward William Morley (1838–1923) Scientists who jointly received the Nobel prize in physics in 1907 for this experiment, which paved the way for the theory of relativity.

MIDAS TOUCH The knack of profiting from whatever one does.

Midas In Greek mythology, a Phrygian king granted the power of turning everything that he touched into gold. Phrygia was an ancient country of Asia Minor settled in the 13th century B.C.

MILLERITE A follower of the teachings of William Miller.

William Miller (*1782–1849*)   A U.S. preacher who declared that the end of the world and the second coming of Christ would occur in 1843.

MILLERITE   A native nickel sulfide, a brassy-yellow crystalline mineral.

William Hallowes Miller (*1801–1880*)   A 19th-century mineralogist (no relation to the preacher) who developed a system of crystallography still in common use, set forth in his *Treatise on Crystallography* (1838).

MILTONIC   Like John Milton or his writings; solemn, elevated, majestic.

John Milton (*1608–1674*)   The author of *Paradise Lost*. Born in London, educated at Christ's College, Cambridge, where he wrote his first poem, he returned to London to act as tutor for his nephews Edward and John Phillips. He began to publish pamphlets against the church, including *Reformation of Church Discipline in England*, which appeared in 1641 and endeared him to very few. By 1664 he had completed *Paradise Lost*, which was published in 10 volumes, later enlarged to 12 books. In the first 18 months 1,300 copies were sold. Milton died as a result of attacks of gout. He is buried beside his father at Cripplegate, London.

MINIÉ BALL   A rifle bullet with a hollow bore.

Captain Claude Etienne Minié **(1814–1879)** French army officer, also the inventor of a rifle, as well as the conical bullet, which bear his name.

MÖBIUS STRIP A surface with only one side, formed by giving a half twist to a narrow, rectangular strip of paper, and then pasting its two ends together.

A. F. Möbius **(1790–1868)** A German mathematician and astronomer, who invented the Möbius strip, whose application is chiefly in mathematics.

MOCHA A rich, pungent Arabian coffee.

Mocha A seaport of Yemen where this coffee originated.

MOHS' SCALE An arbitrary scale used to indicate the relative hardness of minerals and stones.

Friedrich Mohs **(1773–1839)** A German mineralogist who introduced the scale of hardness which is commonly used today.

MOLOCH Anything demanding terrible sacrifice.

Moloch In the Hebrew Bible, an ancient Phoenician and Ammonite god to whom children were sacrificed by burning.

MOLOTOV COCKTAIL   A bottle filled with gasoline, wrapped in a saturated rag or plugged with a wick, ignited, and hurled as a grenade.

V. M. Molotov (1890–1986)   Soviet statesman and foreign minister of the U.S.S.R. 1939–1949 and 1953–1956. The Molotov cocktail probably was named for him because he was prominent in the October Revolution in 1917. He was a close associate of Lenin, a member of the Politburo, and secretary of the central committee of the Communist party in 1922, president from 1930–1941, and held many other important government posts.

MOMUS   One who finds fault, a critic of petty details.

Momus   In Greek mythology, the god of blame and ridicule.

MORGAN   Any of a breed of strong, light harness or saddle horses.

Justin Morgan (1747–1798)   New Englander who owned the sire of the breed; his name and the breed have been perpetuated ever since.

MORGANITE   A transparent rose-colored variety of beryl, used as a gem.

J. P. Morgan (1837–1913)   A famous American banker and financier who formed the J. P. Morgan

Co. in 1895 and the U.S. Steel Company in 1901. He is best known for his reorganization of important American railroads and for his industrial consolidations. He was also a collector of art and rare books, president of the Metropolitan Museum of Art in New York City, benefactor of the Cathedral of St. John the Divine, the Metropolitan Museum of Art, New York Public Library, and many other institutions.

MOROCCO A fine, soft leather made from goatskins tanned with sumac.

Morocco A kingdom on the northwest coast of Africa where morocco leather was originally made.

MORPHINE A derivative of opium used in medicine to relieve pain, allowing a patient to rest and sleep.

Morpheus In Greek mythology, the god of dreams.

MORRIS CHAIR An armchair with an adjustable back and removable cushions.

William Morris (1834–1896) An eminent English poet and artist, one of the originators of *Oxford and Cambridge Magazine,* through which he became a good friend of Dante Gabriel Rossetti. In addition, he studied the practical art of dyeing and carpet weaving and founded the Society for the Protection of Ancient Buildings. He also added typography to his many activities and started the Kelmscot Press in 1890 at Hammersmith, for which he designed special type and ornamental letters and borders for use in publishing medieval French romances. He published many volumes of his own verse, and produced many illuminated manuscripts, including two of FitzGerald's *Omar Khayyam*. One of the leaders of the Romantic school, Morris was considered a disciple of beauty for beauty's sake. He designed, used, and liked the Morris chair.

MORSE CODE A system of dots and dashes, or short and long sounds or flashes, used to represent letters, etc., in telegraphy.

Samuel Morse (1791–1872) The inventor of the telegraph and the Morse code. He became interested in the possibilities of magnetic telegraphy as early as 1832. In 1843 the U.S. Congress voted him $30,000 for an experimental line between Washington and Baltimore. The first message sent over this line was "What hath God wrought!" Morse was involved in a great deal of litigation over rights to his inventions during his lifetime, but the courts upheld him and he enjoyed prosperity in his later years. A statue of him stands in New York City's Central Park. He is a member of the American Hall of Fame.

MOTHER HUBBARD   A woman's long, loose un-belted dress.

Mother Hubbard   The title of a well-known nursery rhyme.

MURPHY BED   A bed that swings up and folds away into a closet or cabinet when not in use.

W. L. Murphy (1876–1950)   Inventor of the Murphy bed (circa 1900). This bed was a real boon in small apartments. Various forms of folding beds (but not ones that disappeared into closets) were displayed at the Philadelphia centennial exposition in 1876 and General Washington used a portable folding cot during the American Revolution, but it was Murphy's ingenious idea of getting rid of the bed entirely in a closet which made his name.

MURPHY'S LAW   A facetious or satirical proposition stating that if there is a possibility for something to go wrong, it will.

E. A. Murphy, Jr.   U.S. engineer who formulated the original version (1949).

MUSEUM   An institution, room, or building for preserving and exhibiting artistic, historic, or scientific objects.

The Muses   In Greek mythology, the nine goddesses who presided over literature and the arts and sciences: Calliope, Clio, Euterpe, Melpomene, Terpsichore, Erato, Polyhymnia, Urania and Thalia. The first places called museums were temples to the Muses. Later, a museum became a kind of study or library. The first museums of the modern type were established during the Renaissance, about six hundred years ago, when people revived their interest in the arts and sciences. Noblemen began to store their collections of ancient statues and paintings in special buildings called museums. Later they were taken over by governments and opened to the public.

N

NAPIER'S BONES   Cubes made out of bone, ivory, or boxwood with numerical tables on their sides.
   John Napier (1550–1617)   The laird of Merchiston Castle, near Edinburgh, Scotland, who invented these mechanical devices for computing in order to reduce the labor of mathematical calculations. Earlier, he had invented logarithms.

NAPOLEONIC CODE   The body of French civil law enacted in 1804; the model for the civil codes of many nations.

Napoleon I, Bonaparte (1769–1821) Emperor of the French from 1804 to 1815.

NARCISSISM Self-love; excessive interest in one's own appearance, comfort, importance, abilities, etc.

Narcissus In Greek mythology, a beautiful youth who, after his lover's death (see ECHO), was made to pine away for love of his own reflection in a pool, and changed into the narcissus flower.

NEGUS A beverage of hot water, wine, and lemon juice, sweetened and spiced.

Colonel Francis Negus (d. 1732) Inventor of the beverage on one cold winter's night when he had too much company and not enough wine to go around. A man who rose to any occasion, he made do with what was on hand to everyone's delight, and the "Negus" was born.

NEMESIS Anyone or anything by which, it seems, one must inevitably be defeated or frustrated.

Nemesis In Greek mythology, Nemesis is the goddess of retributive justice, or vengeance.

NERETIC Of or pertaining to the waters and deposits of a shoreline.

Nereus In Greek mythology, a sea god, father of the Nereids.

NEROLI An essential oil distilled from orange flowers and used in perfume. Also called "neroli oil," "orange flower oil."

The Princess of Neroli, Anna Maria de la Tremoille The woman who introduced it into France in about 1680.

NERONIAN Displaying a disposition to cruelty, tyranny, or depravity comparable to that of the emperor.

Nero, Claudius Caesar Drusus Germanicus (A.D. 37–68) Roman emperor who instituted cruel persecutions of Christians. He led a private life of dissipation, murdered his wife Octavia and her sister Antonia, married Poppaea Sabina (62) and later caused her death, accused of kindling a fire that destroyed a great part of Rome (64), assassinated his mother (59) and brought about the deaths of many Romans, including Seneca, one of his chief advisors. He was finally declared a public enemy by the Senate, and committed suicide.

NESSELRODE A mixture, often rum-flavored, of chestnuts, oranges, cherries, and other dried fruits used in puddings, ice creams, or pies.

Count Karl von Nesselrode (1780–1862) A Russian statesman on the staff of the diplomatic corps of Alexander I in the negotiations following the fall of Napoleon. In 1816 he was Russian minister of foreign affairs, vice-chancellor in 1829, and chancellor in 1844. He concluded the Treaty of Paris after the Crimean War (1854–1856) and then retired, presumably to enjoy more of the scrumptious meals made by his excellent chef (name unknown) who whipped up *nesselrode* one day, and cleverly named it after his illustrious boss.

NESTOR   A venerable and wise old man.

Nestor   In Homeric poems, a hero celebrated for his age and the wisdom of his counsel.

NEWBERY MEDAL   Prize annually awarded since 1921 for the most distinguished contribution to literature for children from the pen of an American writer.

John Newbery (1713–1767)   English publisher who set up his bookshop and publishing house in St. Paul's Churchyard in 1744 and published *Mother Goose's Nursery Rhymes* (c. 1760), as well as other children's books such as *Goody Two Shoes, Tommy Trip, Giles Gingerbread,* etc.

NICOL PRISM   A prism consisting of two crystals.

William Nicol (1768?–1851)   A British physicist who invented the Nicol prism in 1828 for producing and analyzing polarized light.

NICOTINE   A poisonous water-soluble alkaloid.

Jean Nicot (1530?–1600)   The French ambassador at Lisbon, Portugal, who first introduced tobacco into France (1560). The terms nicotine and *Nicotiana* (genus to which the tobacco plant belongs) derive from his name.

NIGHTINGALE   A caring person, a nurse.

Florence Nightingale (1820–1910)   English nurse known as "the lady with the lamp." She was born in Florence, Italy, of wealthy parents. After nursing training, she took 38 nurses to the battlefields of the Crimean war and organized a barracks hospital. She introduced sanitation, decreased the number of cases of typhus, cholera, and dysentery, and founded an institution for the training of nurses in 1868. Florence Nightingale was the first woman to receive Great Britain's Order of Merit in 1907, and is regarded as the founder of modern nursing.

NIMROD   A hunter.

Nimrod   The grandson of Noah, described in the Bible as "a mighty hunter before the lord" (Genesis 10:8–10).

NIOBIUM   An element.

Niobe   In Greek mythology, the daughter of Tantalus. Because the element niobium is extracted from tantalum, the element named after Tantalus, it was given the name of his daughter.

NOBELIST A person who receives a Nobel prize.

Alfred Bernhard Nobel (1833–1896) Swedish manufacturer, inventor, and philanthropist. He really did care about people despite the fact that he invented dynamite (1866), balliestite, one of the first smokeless powders (1888), artificial gutta percha, and over 100 other patented items. His enormous wealth, however, was mainly acquired through the manufacture of dynamite and other explosives in various parts of the world. In 1901 he bequeathed a fund of $9,200,000 for the establishment of the Nobel prizes—oddly, one of the main categories is "for promoting peace." The prizes are also given annually for distinction in physics, chemistry, economics, physiology, and literature.

O

OCEAN The great body of salt water that covers approximately 71 percent of the earth's surface.

Oceanus In Greek mythology, a Titan who was god of the sea before Poseidon and father of the

Oceanids, who were any of three thousand ocean nymphs.

OCKHAM or OCCAM'S RAZOR   A philosophical or scientific principle according to which the best explanation of an event is the one that is the simplest, using the fewest assumptions, hypotheses, etc.

William of Ockham (1285?–1349)   English scholastic philosopher, and a rival of Duns Scotus (see DUNCE). He practically closed the scholastic controversy over universals with his doctrine that the real is always individual, not universal, and that universals have no real existence but are only abstract terms, and the corollary that "entities must not be unnecessarily multiplied," which is called Occam's Razor.

ODYSSEY   An extended adventurous wandering.

Odyssey   The second epic of Homer, which recounts the wanderings of Odysseus after the fall of Troy, and his eventual return home.

OEDIPUS COMPLEX   The tendency of a child to be attached to the parent of the opposite sex and hostile toward the other parent.

Oedipus   King of Thebes, a figure in Greek mythology. Abandoned at birth, he grew to manhood unaware of his true parentage and unwittingly killed his father and married his mother. Thus the complex, in which a male child has a strong attachment for his mother, accompanied by hostility toward the father.

OHM   A unit of electrical resistance.

George Simon Ohm (1787–1854)   A German physicist who discovered the relationship between the strength or intensity of an unvarying electrical current, the electromotive force, and the resistance of a circuit, now known as Ohm's law.

OLYMPIAD   The interval of four years between celebrations of the Olympic games, by which the ancient Greeks recorded dates.

OLYMPIAN   A contestant in the Olympic games; of or pertaining to the gods of the ancient Greek pantheon, whose home was Mount Olympus; of or pertaining to the Olympic games.

Olympia   A plain in ancient Elis, Peloponnesus, site of the ancient Olympic games in Greece.

ONANISM   Withdrawal in sexual intercourse before ejaculation; also masturbation.

Onan   Son of Judah (Genesis 38:9).

ORPHIC   Capable of casting a spell or charm.

Orpheus The legendary Thracian poet whose singing cast such a spell and to whom the establishment of the Orphic mysteries was ascribed.

ORWELLIAN Referring to the practice of intellectual dishonesty in the service of totalitarian rule.

George Orwell (1903–1950) Pen name of Eric Blair, author who described a totalitarian society in his famous book *1984.*

P

PALLADIUM A sacred object having the power to preserve a city or state possessing it; a safeguard.

Pallas Another name for Athena, the goddess of wisdom, also called Pallas Athena. In ancient Greece and Rome statues called "palladia" (plural of "palladium") were erected of the Greek goddess Pallas Athena, specifically the legendary statue in Troy, on the preservation of which the safety of the city was supposed to depend.

PALMER METHOD A handwriting script widely taught in American public schools at the beginning of the 20th century.

Austin Norman Palmer (1859–1927) American penman and educator, originator of the method of handwriting taught widely in public schools.

PANAMA HAT A natural-colored, hand-plaited hat made from the leaves of the jipijapa plant of South and Central America.

Panama A republic of Central America, 28,575 sq. miles in area, on the Isthmus of Panama, where the Panama hat was first made.

PANDERER A go-between in sexual intrigue; one who caters to the lower tastes and desires of others to exploit their weaknesses.

Pandare A character in Chaucer's *Troilus and Criseyde* who procures Criseyde's love for Troilus; name taken from Pandaro in Boccaccio's *Filostrata;* Pandarus, in the *Aeneid;* Pandaros, in the *Iliad.*

PANDORA'S BOX Anything that causes unexpected troubles or difficulties when opened or broached.

Pandora In Greek mythology, the first mortal woman, who in curiosity opened a box, letting all human ills out into the world, or, in a later version, letting all human blessings escape and be lost, leaving only hope.

PANIC   A sudden, overpowering terror.

Pan   The god of woods, fields, and flocks, having a human torso with goat's legs, horns, and ears. He lends his name to panic because he would arouse terror in lonely places.

PANPIPE   A primitive wind instrument consisting of a series of pipes or reeds of graduated length bound together and played by blowing across the top open ends. Also called "mouth organ."

Pan   The god of the woods, fields, and flocks who goes about happily playing his pipes. (See PANIC.)

PANTALOONS   Formerly, men's tight trousers extending from waist to ankle. Later, any kind of trousers.

Pantaloon   A stock character in old Italian comedy, the butt of the clown's jokes. From the Venetian patron saint Pantalone or Pantaleone, this stock character was usually a slender, foolish old man wearing tight trousers extending to the feet.

PAP TEST   A test for determining cervical cancer.

George Papanicolaou (1883–1962)   U.S. anatomist who developed the test, which is credited with saving many thousands of lives.

PARKINSON'S DISEASE A degenerative disease, characterized by a rhythmic tremor and muscular rigidity, caused by degeneration in the basal ganglia of the brain.

James Parkinson (1755–1824) English surgeon and paleontologist who wrote the first article on appendicitis (1812) and was the first to recognize perforation as a cause of death. He described Parkinson's disease in 1817. He is the author of many medical books.

PARKINSON'S LAW Any of several satirical statements expressed as economic laws, as one to the effect that work expands to fill the time allotted.

C. Northcote Parkinson (b. 1909) Author of the book *Parkinson's Law*, who became world-famous after its publication.

-PAROUS Combining form meaning producing, giving birth.

Parcae In Roman mythology, the birth goddesses (singular *parca*). These goddesses are: Atropos, who carries the shears and cuts the thread of life; Clotho, who carries the spindle and spins the thread of life; and Lachesis who carries the globe or scroll and determines the length of the thread of life. They are also known as the three Fates.

PARSONS TABLE A lightweight, square-legged table of geometric design with no exposed joints, now often made of molded plastic.

Parsons School of Design School in New York noted for its innovative design concepts.

PASTEURIZATION A method of destroying disease-producing bacteria and checking the activity of fermentative bacteria, as in milk, beer, cider, etc., by heating the liquid to a prescribed temperature for a specified period of time.

PASTEURIZE To subject to pasteurization

Louis Pasteur (1822–1895) A French chemist, professor of chemistry at the Sorbonne from 1867 to 1889, and director of the Institut Pasteur in Paris. He demonstrated that lactic, alcoholic, and other fermentations are caused by minute organisms and proved these organisms do not arise by spontaneous generation. In addition to his pioneering work in destroying disease-causing bacteria in milk and other liquids, he discovered the germs causing diseases of silkworms and found a method of preventing them, thus saving the silk industry in France. He also developed curative and preventive treatment for hydrophobia in man and for rabies in dogs and used his treatment successfully on a child bitten by a mad dog in 1885.

PEACH MELBA Peach halves, vanilla ice cream, and a sauce of raspberries and currants.

Nellie Melba (1861–1931) Internationally famous opera singer of the early 20th century (See MELBA TOAST).

PECKSNIFFIAN Falsely moralistic, hypocritical, insincere.

Pecksniff An unctuous hypocrite in Charles Dickens' *Martin Chuzzlewit*.

PECOS BILL In American folklore, a legendary frontier cowboy who performed such superhuman feats as digging the Rio Grande.

Pecos Native name of a river in the southwest U.S., flowing from New Mexico through Texas into the Rio Grande.

PEELER Slang name for a British policeman. (See BOBBY.)

Sir Robert Peel (1788–1850) British statesman and prime minister. As Home Secretary he organized the Metropolitan Police Force in 1828.

PEEPING TOM A person who gets pleasure, especially sexual pleasure, from watching others, especially furtively.

Tom (last name unknown) In English legend, the Coventry tailor who was struck blind after peeping at Lady Godiva, when she rode nude through the streets of the city. This 11th-century woman did so, according to legend, on the dare of her husband so that he would abolish a heavy tax.

PERICLEAN Refers to a period of great commercial, intellectual, and artistic achievement in Athens.

Pericles (*495?–429 b.c.*) Athenian statesman and general. While preparing Athens for the inevitable conflict with Sparta (see SPARTAN), he strove also to make the city the center of art and literature and architecturally the most beautiful city in the world. Pericles was responsible for building, the Parthenon, Propylaea, Odeon, and other noted buildings, and he gathered about himself groups of prominent people. His conduct of the Peloponnesian War which began in 431 b.c. was vigorous.

PETER PRINCIPLE, THE The satirical proposition that each employee in an organization tends to be promoted until he reaches his level of incompetence.

L. J. Peter & R. Hull Authors of the book of the same name (1968).

PETRI DISH A very shallow, cylindrical transparent glass or plastic dish with an overlapping cover, used for culture of microorganisms.

Julius R. Petri (1852–1921)   German bacteriologist.

PHILIPPIC   Any bitter verbal attack.

King Philip of Macedon (382–336 B.C.)   Conqueror who made Macedon an important empire of the ancient world. He seized the throne at age twenty-three, built up a strong army, and conquered and ruled all of Greece. When Philip's ships began to interfere seriously with the Athenians' trade routes, an anti-Philip group understandably began to grow in Athens, under the leadership of the incomparable orator Demosthenes. An expert lawyer, Demosthenes delivered the first Philippic, an impassioned appeal to the Athenians to realize their danger from Philip, and to counteract that danger by crafting a standing naval and military force. In this first of three famous Philippic orations, Demosthenes presented proposals that, had the Athenians paid attention and followed them, might have saved Athens and Greece from Philip's claws. Philip is also famous for being the father of Alexander the Great.

PHILOMEL   A nightingale.

Philomela   In Greek mythology, a princess of Athens whom the gods turned into a nightingale after she was raped by Tereus, husband of her sister Procne. Tereus was changed into a hawk and Procne into a sparrow.

PHOENIX   A symbol of immortality.

Phoenix   In Egyptian mythology, a bird that consumed itself by fire after 500 years, and rose renewed from its ashes.

PHRYGIAN CAP   A cap with a forward-curving peak, represented in ancient Greek art as part of the attire worn by Phrygians.

Phrygia   An ancient country of west-central Asia Minor, settled in the 13th century B.C.

PICKLE   Any brine, vinegar, or spicy solution used to preserve or marinate food; any edible product such as a cucumber thus preserved.

William Beukel (d. 1397)   The Dutchman who pickled the first fish in 14th-century Holland. The process and the product were originally called beckle, but became corrupted to its present form over the years. After fish, he tried cucumbers with equal success.

PICKWICKIAN   Of or characteristic of Mr. Pickwick or the Pickwick Club; used with a special or esoteric sense: said of a word or phrase; learned, but amiable and innocent.

Mr. Samuel Pickwick   The naive, benevolent president of the Pickwick Club in Dickens' *Pickwick Papers* (1836).

PIERROT COLLAR   Smaller version of the large stiff ruffled collar worn by the character Pierrot.

Pierrot   A French pantomime character dressed in a floppy white outfit and a wide, ruffled collar.

PINCHBECK   An alloy of zinc and copper used as imitation gold; a cheap imitation, spurious.

Christopher Pinchbeck (1670–1732)   English jeweller who invented the alloy. He made mechanical singing birds, barrel organs, musical clocks, and watches of all sorts from this alloy of copper and zinc which closely resembled gold and which, from time to time, Christopher sold as the real thing. In July 8, 1721, an announcement appeared in *Applebee's Weekly Journal.* It read: "Christopher Pinchbeck, inventor and maker of the famous astronomico-music clock, is removed ... to the sign of the 'Astronomico-Musical Clock' in Fleet Street, near the Leg Tavern. He maketh and selleth watches of all sorts, and clocks, as well plain, for the exact indication of time only, as astronomical, for showing the various motions and phenomena of planets and fixed stars." A most boastful fellow, this Pinchbeck!

PINDARIC   Characteristic of or in the style of Pindar.

Pindar (522–438? B.C.)   A Greek lyric poet. "Pindaric" designates an ode in which the strophe and antistrophe have the same form, in contrast to the epode, which has a different form. Strophe, antistrophe, and epode refer to metrical patterns in the verses.

PLANCK'S CONSTANT   In physics, a universal constant.

Max Planck (1858–1947)   Scientist who was awarded the Nobel prize for physics in 1918. He is known also for work related to thermodynamics and mechanics and to electrical and optical problems associated with radiation of heat and, of course, his famous quantum theory.

PLATONIC   Now used to designate a relationship between a man and a woman that is purely spiritual or intellectual and without sexual activity.

Plato   Greek philosopher, disciple of Socrates and teacher of Aristotle. His original name was Aristocles but he was surnamed Plato because of his broad shoulders. He wrote *The Symposium,* a dialogue on ideal love in which the participants, including Socrates, Aristophanes, and Alcibiades, discuss the nature of love.

PLIMSOLL   A lightweight canvas shoe with rubber soles; a sneaker. So-called probably from some fancied resemblance to a Plimsoll mark.

Samuel Plimsoll (*1824–1898*)   British advocate of legislation against overloading vessels. A line or set of lines on the outside of merchant ships, showing the water level to which they may legally be loaded, was called a Plimsoll mark. The mudguard of a sneaker resembles the Plimsoll mark.

PLUMERIA   A fragrant flowering tree of Hawaii whose white or golden blossoms are used in the making of leis, a wreath of flowers and leaves worn around the neck.

Charles Plumier (*1646–1706*)   Distinguished French botanist. He originally intended to become a mathematician, but gave it up for botany in his youth. In 1689 at the request of Louis XIV, Plumier agreed to accompany a physician from Marseilles named Joseph Surian on a voyage to the Caribbean. Their intention was to discover medical applications for the plants they gathered—Surian to make the chemical analyses while Plumier gathered the collections. The two men quarreled. On a second voyage in 1693, Plumier traveled alone. Upon his return he published an elaborate book describing the plants of the Americas, which included 107 plates engraved at Louis XIV's expense. In 1695 he set out on a third expedition to Guadeloupe, Martinique, Santo Domingo, and the southern coast of Brazil. After the trip, he wrote two important books which contained many elaborate plates and descriptions of 106 new genera, among them the plumeria, which Louis allowed him to name for himself. In 1704 Plumier decided to sail to Peru in search of the cinchona tree (from the bark of which quinine and other medicines are obtained). While waiting for the ship to sail, he died, probably from pneumonia. His drawings of plants and Surian's analyses of their medical properties on which they collaborated still exist. (See CHINCHONA.)

PLUTONIAN   The infernal regions.

Pluto   In Greek and Roman mythology, the god ruling over the lower world, also called *Hades* by the Greeks and *Dis* or *Orcus* by the Romans.

POINCIANA   Any of a genus *Poinciana* of small tropical trees and shrubs of the legume family, growing in dry, sandy soil and having showy red, orange, or yellow flowers.

M. de Poinci   Early governor of the French West Indies who first called the colorful plant to the attention of botanists.

POINSETTIA   A Mexican and Central American plant with yellow flowers surrounded by tapering red leaves resembling petals.

Joel R. Poinci (d. 1851)   The U.S. ambassador to Mexico. He was impressed by the showy, red-leaved

183

plant which bloomed there in the winter. He brought it to the attention of botanists, who were equally impressed and delighted and honored him by naming the exotic discovery after him.

POLLYANNA   A foolishly optimistic person.

Pollyanna   A character in the 1913 novel of the same name written by Eleanor Porter (1868–1920).

POMERANIAN   A breed of small dogs having long, silky hair.

Pomerania   A historic region of north-central Europe, extending along the south coast of the Baltic Sea, now divided between Poland and East Germany.

POMPADOUR   A woman's hair style formed by sweeping the hair straight up from the forehead.

Marquise de Pompadour, Jeanne Antoinette Poisson (1721–1764)   The mistress of Louis XV of France; it was said that she controlled him completely. Among her many unpopular (and rash) political decisions was changing Richelieu's purpose of weakening the house of Austria to one of alliances with Austria. This brought on the Seven Years' War (1756–1763), which was disastrous to France.

POTT'S DISEASE   Tuberculosis of the vertebrae causing curvature of the spine.

Percival Pott (1714–1788) English surgeon credited with introducing many improvements to make surgery more humane. He took steps to abolish extensive use of caustic substances and the painful practice of cauterizing a wound. He is notable for having given the first clinical description of the spinal affliction known as *Pott's Disease.*

PRALINE Any of various concoctions made of nuts, sugar, etc., as a crisp candy made of a pecan, almond, etc. browned in boiling sugar; a soft or crisp candy patty made of pecans and brown sugar, maple syrup, etc.

Marshal Duplessis-Praslin (1598–1675) The man whose cook is said to have invented it for a particularly important dinner party; it was a great success as an unusual dessert.

PRIAPIC Phallic. **PRIAPISM** Persistent, usually painful, erection of the penis, especially as a consequence of disease.

Priapus The Greco-Roman god of procreation, guardian of gardens and vineyards, and personification of the erect phallus.

PRIVATE EYE A detective.

The Pinkerton Detective Agency A company, headed by Alan Pinkerton (1819–1894), a U.S. detective born in Scotland, which featured a large eye on its letterhead. Since all the detective work they did was "private," the term "private eye" came into being, originally designating the Pinkertons only, and then others. (See FINK.)

PROCRUSTEAN Producing conformity by ruthless or arbitrary means.

Procrustes In Greek mythology, a fabulous Greek giant who either stretched or shortened his captives to fit one of his iron beds. To shorten the tall ones, Procrustes would cut their legs off.

PROMETHEAN Life-giving, creative, or courageously original.

Prometheus In Greek mythology, a Titan who stole fire from heaven for the benefit of mankind; in punishment Zeus chained him to a rock where a vulture came each day to eat his liver, which Zeus renewed every night.

PROTEAN Readily taking on different shapes or forms, variable, versatile.

Proteus A Greek sea god who had the power to change his shape.

PSYCHE The human soul.

Psyche In Roman mythology, a maiden who—after undergoing many hardships due to Venus's jealousy of her beauty—is reunited with Cupid and made immortal by Jupiter. There are many derivatives of psyche, including psychology, psychic, psychedelic, psychoanalyze, psychodrama, psychosis, and psychopath.

PTOLEMAIC SYSTEM The theory that the earth is the center or fixed point of the universe, around which the heavenly bodies move.

Ptolemy (2nd century A.D.) Alexandrian astronomer, mathematician, and geographer. His theory of the universe was widely accepted for hundreds of years.

PULLMAN A railroad car with private compartments or seats that can be made up into berths for sleeping. Also, Pullman kitchen, a small compact kitchen typically built into an alcove, as in some apartments.

George M. Pullman (1831–1897) A cabinetmaker who decided that the sleeping cars of his time could be improved. The typical sleeping car was equipped with bunks and lumpy mattresses. There were no blankets or pillows or sheets. Passengers lay down fully clothed. Washing facilities consisted of a community towel and a pitcher of cold water. Pullman and a friend set to work converting two trains

187

of the Chicago and Alton Railroad into sleeping cars. When the first two were completed, George realized he would need money to expand. So he went in search of gold. He didn't find it, but he returned to Chicago with $20,000 from a mysterious investor, which allowed him to continue his work. With his good friend Ben Field he patented his Pullman car with folding upper berth in 1864. In 1865 he extended seat cushions to make lower berths. When railroads began accepting these cars, he organized the Pullman Palace Car Co. in 1867. He also devised dining cars in 1868, chair cars in 1875, and vestibule cars in 1887.

PUNCH, PLEASED AS Highly pleased, gratified.

Punch The quarrelsome hook-nosed husband of Judy in the comic puppet show, *Punch and Judy.* (Punch is short for Punchinello).

PYRRHIC VICTORY A too costly victory.

Pyrrhus (318?–272 B.C.) King of Epirus, who was involved in two victories over the Romans which were achieved at such staggering cost that it amounted to no victory at all. The first was in 280 B.C. and the second in 279 B.C. Pyrrhus is quoted as saying, "One more such victory, and I am ruined."

PYTHIAN Pertaining to Delphi, the temple of Apollo at Delphi, or its oracle; mysterious.

Pythia The oracular priestess of Apollo at Delphi. (See DELPHIC.)

Q

QUASSIA TREE A tropical tree from the wood or bark of which is obtained a bitter substance used in medicine and as an insecticide.

Graman Quassi An 18th-century black slave of Suriname (formerly Dutch Guiana) who discovered the value of the bark and wood of these trees in the treatment of malignant fevers which were common in Suriname. In honor of this discovery, the great botanist Linnaeus gave the name *Quassi* to the genus.

QUEENSBERRY RULES A boxing code of fair play developed in 1865 covering the basic rules of modern boxing, providing for the use of gloves, the division of a match into rounds, etc.

The 8th Marquess of Queensberry (1844–1900) English nobleman who supervised the formulation of the code.

QUISLING A traitor.

189

Vidkun Quisling (1887–1945)   A Norwegian politician and official, he founded his own political party, the National Union, with a platform calling for the suppression of Communism and the freeing of Norwegian labor from unionism. As head of Norway's government in 1940 he collaborated in the German conquest of the country. As a result his name has become a synonym for traitor.

QUIXOTIC   Caught up in the romance of noble deeds or unreachable ideals.

Don Quixote   Title character in the Spanish novel *Don Quixote;* he was the personification of romance without regard to practicality. This satirical novel by Cervantes was published in two parts in 1605 and 1615 featuring a hero who tries in a chivalrous but unrealistic way to rescue the oppressed and fight evil.

R

RABELAISIAN   Broadly and coarsely humorous, satirical, etc.

François Rabelais (1494–1553)   French satirist and humorist who was a monk, a member of the Cordelier convent of Fontenay-le-Comte. He studied medicine at Montpellier (1530) and practiced at Lyons (1532). He wandered widely in France and Italy, then returned to take the parish of Meudon. He edited various medical treatises but his fame is due to two novels, published under the pseudonym Alcofribas Nasier (an anagram of his real name). They were *Pantagruel* (1533) and *Gargantua* (1535); both were noted for their broad and racy humor and grotesque invention.

RAGLAN A loose overcoat or topcoat with sleeves that continue in one piece to the collar, so that there are no seams at the shoulder.

Lord Raglan, Fitzroy James Henry Somerset (1788–1855) British lord who, as a twenty-seven-year-old lieutenant colonel serving with the Duke of Wellington, lost his right arm on the eve of the Battle of Waterloo, the victim of a sniper's bullet. As a result he wore a large, billowing, black coat with loose and wide sleeves on, and off, the battlefield. The coat became so identified with him that his men called it a "raglan." Lord Raglan was much admired for his bravery and he had a long and distinguished military career, despite his handicap. He was military secretary from 1812–1814; secretary to Wellington from 1818–52; succeeded Wellington as commander of forces and was created a Baron in 1852. He commanded the British troops in the Crimean War; won the battle of Alma in 1854; blamed Lucan for the loss of the light brigade at Balaklava (1854); and was made a scapegoat for the failure of the commissariat during the winter of 1854–1855. He died ten days after the repulse at Malakoff and Redan.

RAMAN EFFECT The alteration in frequency and random alteration in phases of light scattered in a material medium.

Sir Chandrasekhara Venkata Raman (1888–1969) Indian physicist and professor at Calcutta University from 1917 to 1933. He was knighted in 1929 and was awarded the Nobel prize in physics in 1930 for his important discoveries.

REMINGTON A rifle.

Eliphalet Remington (1793–1861) Manufacturer of firearms. His factory for making rifles was established in what is now Ilion, New York, in 1828. He also marketed the Remington pistol from about 1847 but it was the rifle which made him and his son, Philo, famous. Later, they expanded into Remington sewing machines and Remington typewriters but were forced by financial conditions to sell both these businesses.

REUBEN SANDWICH A sandwich made with rye bread, filled usually with corned beef, sauerkraut, Swiss cheese, and dressing, and served hot.

Reuben Kay   Omaha grocer who first concocted the sandwich, circa 1930.

REYE'S SYNDROME   A rare, often fatal disease, usually of children, cause unknown. It most frequently occurs after a viral illness, such as influenza.

R. D. Reye   Australian pathologist who first described the illness in 1963.

REYNOLDS NUMBER   A nondimensional parameter used to determine the nature of fluid flow along surfaces and around objects, such as in a wind tunnel.

Osborne Reynolds (1843–1912)   English physicist who devised it.

RHINESTONE   A colorless, bright, artificial gem made of hard glass, often cut in imitation of a diamond.

Strasbourg on the Rhine   Region where the stones were originally made.

RHODES SCHOLAR   Recipient of a scholarship for a two-year or three-year period of study at Oxford University.

Cecil Rhodes (1853–1901)   British financier and colonial administrator in South Africa. He acquired his fortune in the Kimberley Diamond Field, and established the Rhodes scholarships in his will. He left $6,000,000 for scholarships for British Commonwealth, German, and American youth.

RICHTER SCALE   A scale by which the magnitude of earthquakes is measured.

C. Richter (1900–1985)   U.S. seismologist who devised the scale.

RITZY   Elegant, fancy, fashionable.

César Ritz (1850–1918)   A Swiss hotelier whose hotels were so elegant, fancy, fashionable (and profitable) that his name soon became a synonym for grandeur and elegance. He founded the Ritz hotels—the jewel in his famous chain being the Ritz-Carlton in New York City. Ritz is immortalized in the great Irving Berlin song "Putting On the Ritz," and in *The Diamond as Big as the Ritz,* by F. Scott Fitzgerald, among other books, plays, and songs, not to mention the popular language.

ROB ROY   A cocktail made with Scotch whisky, sweet vermouth, and bitters.

Rob Roy (1671–1734)   A Scottish freebooter (a person who pillages and plunders) whose original name was Robert Macgregor. He was the leader of the clan Macgregor, and hero of legends, particularly in Sir Walter Scott's novel *Rob Roy.*

ROBINSON CRUSOE The hero of Daniel Defoe's novel *Robinson Crusoe,* about a shipwrecked sailor who lived for years on a small tropical island.

Alexander ("Robinson Crusoe") Selkirk **(1676– 1721)** The original of Defoe's hero Robinson Crusoe. He joined William Dampier in a privateering expedition in the South Seas. When he quarreled with his captain he was set ashore in October, 1704, at his own request on Mas-a-Tierra, one of the Juan Fernandez islets, and he remained there alone until he was taken off on February, 1709, by Thomas Dover. (See DOVER'S POWDER.) The story of Alexander Selkirk was probably told to Defoe by Woodes Rogers, commander of the ship which rescued him, since they were friends.

ROLFING Integration of the human structure in the field of gravity; aligning the body parts.

Dr. Ida P. Rolfe **(1895–1985)** A 1920 graduate of Barnard College, Columbia University; she worked at the Rockefeller Institute in the departments of chemotherapy and organic chemistry and was published frequently in the *Journal of Biological Chemistry.* In seeking a means to relieve the human body of stress (backaches, headaches, etc.) she discovered a system of manipulation called "rolfing" which realigns the body.

ROMEO A male lover.

Romeo   The tragic hero of William Shakespeare's *Romeo and Juliet.*

ROME   The capital of Italy, formerly the capital of the Roman republic, the Roman Empire, and the Papal States.

Romulus   In Roman mythology, Romulus was the son of Mars and a vestal virgin. With his twin brother Remus, he was abandoned as an infant to die but was raised by a she-wolf. He later killed Remus, founded Rome in 753 B.C. and became the first king of Rome. As we said—it's all a myth.

RORSCHACH TEST   A psychological projective test of personality in which a subject's interpretations of ten standard abstract designs are analyzed as a measure of emotional and intellectual functioning and integration.

Herman Rorschach (1824–1932)   A Swiss psychiatrist who devised the test.

RUBENESQUE   Referring to a woman's figure that is full, voluptuous, and shapely.

Peter Paul Rubens (1577–1640)   A Flemish artist who immortalized such women.

RUTHERFORD ATOM   An atom with electrons revolving around a small, central positive nucleus that constitutes practically the entire mass of the atom.

Baron Ernest Rutherford (1871–1937) British physicist, who was a professor of physics at McGill University in Montreal, Canada, and later at the University of Manchester; he was director of the Cavendish Laboratory, Cambridge, and was awarded the 1908 Nobel prize for chemistry. He enunciated the theory that the atom is not indivisible and consists of a small impenetrable nucleus.

S

SABIN VACCINE   An oral vaccine to prevent polio.

Albert Bruce Sabin (b. 1906)   U.S. physician and bacteriologist, born in Russia, who developed the test.

SADISM   The getting of sexual pleasure from dominating, mistreating, or hurting one's partner.

Marquis de Sade (1740–1814)   A French soldier whose complete name was the Comte Donatien Alphonse François de Sade, better known as the Marquis de Sade. He was confined most of his life in various prisons, and died in an insane asylum. He was the author of a number of obscene novels including, *Justine* (1791) and *Juliette* (1798). Sadism, a form of sexual perversion in which gratification is obtained by inflicting pain on the loved one, was described by him and receives its name from him.

SAINT AGNES' EVE The night of January 20, when, according to legend, a woman will dream of her future husband.

Saint Agnes (d. A.D. 304) A Roman Catholic child martyr who was beheaded because she refused to marry.

SAINT BERNARD DOG A large, strong dog of a breed developed in Switzerland.

Saint Bernard's Hospice Hospice located in the Swiss Alps. The monks of Saint Bernard's used this dog to patrol the Alps.

SAINT ELMO'S FIRE A visible electric discharge from charged, especially pointed, objects such as the tips of masts, spires, trees, etc., seen sometimes during electrical storms.

Saint Elmo The patron saint of sailors and since the "fire" is usually seen at sea during an electric storm, early seamen named it after their patron saint.

SAINT JOHN'S BREAD The long, blackish, sugary, edible pod of the carob.

St. John Prophet who lived on honey and locusts while preaching; the carob pod got its name through confusion of the locusts with the carob, known also as locust bean (Matthew 3:4).

SAINT VITUS' DANCE   Chorea, a disease which affects the nervous system, causing involuntary jerking movements.

Saint Vitus, also known as Saint Guy (3rd century A.D.)   Patron saint of persons with chorea. Born in Sicily, he converted to Christianity at the age of 7 without his parents' knowledge. Moved by divine inspiration, he escaped to Luciania, Italy, with his nurse Crescentia and his teacher Modestus. From there, they moved to Rome where news of the young miracle-worker reached the ears of Emperor Diocletian. Saint Vitus delivered the emperor's daughter of an evil spirit. But when he wouldn't sacrifice to the gods, his powers were thought to be sorcery. He and his nurse and teacher were thrown into a cauldron of molten lead and pitch. They emerged uninjured. All three were then transferred from Rome back to Lucania by an angel. Nothing is known of his personal history or the circumstances of his martydom.

SALK VACCINE   A vaccine to prevent polio.
Jonas Salk (b. 1914)   U.S. physician and bacteriologist who developed the Salk vaccine.

SALISBURY STEAK   Chopped meat in patty form.

Dr. J. M. Salisbury　A British physician of the 19th-century, who was a great advocate of dietary reform. His original salisbury steak formula included eggs, milk, bread crumbs and other items designed to make the patty more nourishing. Today, of course, it is a kind of chopped steak similar to hamburger, but served in a gravy.

SALLY LUNN　A variety of sweetened tea cake.
　Sally Lunn　An 18th-century woman who is said to have first baked it.

SALMONELLA　A bacteria which causes various diseases in man and domestic animals, including typhoid fever and food poisoning.
　Daniel Elmer Salmon (1850–1914)　An American veterinarian and investigator for the U.S. Department of Agriculture. In 1884 he became chief of the Bureau of Animal Industry. He inaugurated a system of meat inspection, instituted a quarantine period for imported livestock, and set up other methods for suppression of contagious disease of cattle. He was the first to recognize and isolate the bacteria called, after him, salmonella.

SAM BROWNE BELT　A military officer's belt with a diagonal strap across the right shoulder designed to carry the weight of a pistol or sword.

Sir Samuel J. Browne (1824–1901) British general who was born and served in India; he was the inventor of the sword belt which bears his name.

SAMARITAN Anyone who goes to the aid of another.

Samaritan, the Good In the Bible (Luke 10:30–37) the only one who goes to the aid of an injured robbery victim lying beside the road.

SAMSON A man of great strength.

Samson In the Bible, an Israelite judge of extraordinary strength, betrayed to the Philistines by Delilah (Judges 14–16).

SANDAL A shoe consisting of a sole fastened to the foot by thongs or straps.

Sandal The name of a Lydian god who wore such shoes, and an ancient Aegean country of Asia Minor.

SANDWICH Two or more slices of bread with meat, cheese, or other filling placed between them.

The 4th Earl of Sandwich, John Montagu (1718–1792) A diplomat, a lord commissioner of the admiralty, first lord of the admiralty, a principal secretary of state, and otherwise accomplished fellow. (The Sandwich Islands, now Hawaiian Islands, were named after him by Captain Cook.) However, despite all his illustrious deeds, his habit of gambling has led to his everlasting fame. So addicted was he to games of chance that he would not leave the gaming tables to eat. So his servants placed a slab of meat between two pieces of bread and brought it to him at the tables, thereby inventing the "sandwich" and assuring him lasting fame.

SANFORIZE To preshrink cloth permanently by a patented process before making garments.

Sanford L. Cluett (1874–1968) The man who invented sanforizing and named it after himself.

SANSEVIERIA Any of various tropical Old World plants of the genus *Sansevieria* having thick, lance-shaped leaves and often cultivated as a house plant.

Raimondo di Sangro (1710–1771) A learned Neopolitan and Prince of Sanseviro, Italy.

SAPPHIC Designating the rhyme scheme of three five-stress lines followed by a short line.

Sappho 7th-century B.C. Greek lyric poetess of the island of Lesbos, who favored such a rhyme scheme. (See LESBIAN.)

SARDINE Any of various small or half-grown edible herrings or related fishes of the family *Chupeidae*.

Sardinia   The second largest (9,196 sq. miles) island in the Mediterranean.

SATURDAY   The seventh and last day of the week.

Saturn   The Roman god of agriculture, akin to the Greek Titan Cronus. The ancient Roman festival of Saturn, called Saturnalia, held about December 17, is also named for this god. It celebrated the winter solstice with general feasting and revelry.

SATURNINE   Sluggish, gloomy, morose, grave, taciturn.

Saturn   The second largest planet in the solar system. In astrology, people born under the planet's influence are supposedly as described above.

SAUCE MORNAY   A sauce made with fish broth, Parmesan and Gruyère cheese, and butter.

Philippe de Mornay (1549–1623)   A French Protestant leader who invented the sauce for his king, Henry IV. Mornay was Henry's right-hand man until the king converted to Catholicism, then Mornay quickly fell out of favor. But his sauce never did.

SAUTERNE   A delicate, sweet white dessert wine.

Sauternes   A commune in southwestern France where this wine was first made.

SAXOPHONE   Any of a group of keyed woodwind instruments having a single reed, conical bone, and metal body, usually curved.

Antoine Joseph (also known as Adolphe) Sax (1814–1894)   Inventor of the saxophone. Young Adolphe grew up with ten brothers and sisters in Brussels. The son of a maker of musical instruments, the bass clarinet was his favorite. It was while he was trying to improve its tone that he invented the saxophone. Later, with borrowed funds, he established a workshop in Paris where he began making wind instruments. Despite such influential friends as Berlioz, Meyerbeer, Halévy, and Donizetti, he had a difficult time. The Parisians took a dim view of this Belgian upstart. It wasn't until February 3, 1844, many years after his arrival, that Sax invited musicians to a little performance to spur their interest in his instruments. Berlioz had written the score which would feature the saxophone, a B-flat trumpet, a cornet, a bass clarinet, and an "improved bugle." The audience was delighted with the music and the saxophone solo in particular brought great applause. Sax was on his way.

SCHICK TEST   A test to determine immunity to diphtheria.

Bela Schick (1877–1967)   U.S. pediatrician, born in Hungary, who devised the test. Schick was pediatrician-in-chief at Mt. Sinai Hospital in New

York from 1923, and clinical professor of diseases of children at Columbia University from 1936. He was known also for writings on scarlet fever, tuberculosis, nutrition of newborns, childhood diets, and especially for discovering the Schick test.

SCHMIDT SYSTEM   An optical system used in certain wide-angle reflecting telescopes.

B. Schmidt (1879–1935)   German astronomer who invented the system. He was an optical instrument maker who invented the telescope named for him. This instrument is widely used to photograph large sections of the sky because of its large field of view and its fine image definition.

SCOPOLIA   A genus of henbane plants.

Giovanni Antonio Scopoli (1723–1788)   An Italian naturalist who was professor of natural history at Pavia in 1777 and a good friend of Linnaeus, who named after him the genus *Scopolia* which, in turn, gave its name to *scopolamine*, an alkaloid occurring in roots and herbs of this genus and used as a sedative and in truth serum.

SCYLLA AND CHARYBDIS, BETWEEN   A no-win situation.

Scylla and Charybdis   Scylla is a dangerous rock on the Italian side of the Straits of Messina, opposite the whirlpool Charybdis; thus to be between Scylla and Charybdis is to be caught between two perils or evils, neither of which can be evaded without risking the other. In classical Greek mythology both Scylla and Charybdis were personified as female monsters.

SEALYHAM TERRIER A terrier of a breed having a wiry white coat, a long head, and short legs.

Sealyham, Pembrokeshire, Wales Region where these terriers were originally developed.

SEDAN An enclosed chair for one person, carried on poles by two men.

Sir Sanders Duncombe of Sedan English holder of the patent for the sedan chair. If he had been more egotistical it might have been called the "Duncombe." Little is known of Duncombe except that he called his invention the "sedan" after the Italian name *seggietta*, the diminutive of *seggia*, a chair. He received a royal patent in 1634 to be the sole supplier of rental or hackney "sedans" for 14 years, a reward for having imported the chair to England. Sedan chairs were welcomed in England as a relief from the swarm of coaches, then clogging London streets. Duncombe, of course, had lived in Sedan, a city in France on the Meuse River, for many years and that's probably where he got the name. Forever after, he was called Sir Sanders Duncombe of Sedan, not *Sudan*, but *Sedan* after the chair.

SEQUOIA   Evergreen coniferous trees of the U.S. West, also called Big Tree and Redwood.

Sequoya   (*1770?–1843*) Legendary Indian scholar who took the name of George Guess at maturity, from an American trader he believed to be his father. He made a study of his own Cherokee language and succeeded in forming a syllabary which was approved by the Cherokee council and proved effective in teaching thousands of his people to read and write.

SERENDIPITY   An aptitude for making fortunate discoveries accidentally.

The Three Princes of Serendip   A Persian fairy tale in which the princes make such discoveries. Serendipity, the word, was actually coined by Horace Walpole, circa 1754.

SHANGHAI   To kidnap a man for compulsory service aboard a ship, especially after rendering him insensible; to induce or compel someone to do something, especially by fraud or force.

Shanghai   The leading seaport of China. It was the custom to kidnap sailors to man ships going to that city.

SHANTUNG   A heavy silk fabric with a rough, nubby surface, made of spun wild silk.

Shantung   A province of China occupying 59,200 square miles in the east, including the Shantung Peninsula, where the material of that name was manufactured.

SHASTA DAISY   A cultivated variety of *Chrysanthemum maximum* from the Pyrenees, having large, white daisylike flowers.

Mount Shasta   Mountain named by Luther Burbank, who lived in California.

SHERRY   A strong fortified Spanish wine, originally *sherris*.

Xeres, Spain   City, now called Jerez, where sherry was first made. Now the term is applied to any similar wine made elsewhere.

SHIRLEY TEMPLE   A soft drink often served to children, made of grenadine, soda, and sugar, topped with an orange slice and maraschino cherry.

Shirley Temple (b. 1928)   Famous motion picture child star of the 1930s.

SHRAPNEL   An artillery shell filled with an explosive charge and many small metal balls designed to explode in the air over the objective.

Henry Shrapnel (1761–1843)   English artillery officer who invented the shrapnel shell, which was first used successfully at Suriname in 1804. Shrapnel served at Gibraltar, in the West Indies, and with the Duke of York in Flanders, where, during the retreat from Dunkirk, his inventive mind proved useful once again. He observed how the wheels of the guns sank into the sand as the men tried to pull them to the water's edge. He promptly suggested that the wheels be locked so they could be skidded over the sand. This maneuver was a success.

SIDEBURNS The hair on a man's face, just in front of the ears, especially when the rest of the beard is cut off.

Ambrose E. Burnside (1824–1881) Famous American army commander who lent his name to the type of side whiskers he wore. Burnside was a graduate of West Point, a brigadier general, a major general, and eventually in command of the Army of the Potomac in 1862. Later, he became governor of Rhode Island (1866–1869) and U.S. Senator (1875–1881).

SILHOUETTE An outline drawing, especially a profile portrait, filled in with a solid color. Silhouettes are usually cut from black paper and fixed on a light background.

Étienne de Silhouette (1709–1767) French controller general of finance in 1759; he introduced unpopular reforms and incurred the ridicule and hostility of the nobility by his economies and attempts to reduce pensions and privileges. It was to ridicule him and his policies that his nobles gave his name to a mere outline, a profile drawing, a "silhouette."

SIMON PURE   Genuine, real, authentic.

Simon Pure   A character in an 18th-century British play called *A Bold Stroke for a Wife*. The hero has a letter of introduction to a man of substance, which is stolen. The person who steals the letter, a Colonel Feignwell, tricks the wealthy man by pretending to be Simon Pure and succeeds in marrying his beautiful daughter. Then the real hero, Simon Pure, turns up and has a very difficult time indeed in proving his real identity.

SIMONY   The buying and selling of church offices.

Simon Magus   A Samaritan magician referred to in the Bible (Acts 8:9–24) as a person who offered money for instruction in the rite of imparting the Holy Ghost by the laying on of hands. Peter and John, righteously indignant at Simon's offer of money, quickly refused, but the story got around and the buying and selling of sacred things has been known as simony ever since.

SISYPHEAN   Describing an arduous, repetitive task.

Sisyphus In Greek mythology, a cruel king of Corinth condemned forever to roll a huge stone up a hill in Hades, only to have it roll down again on nearing the top.

SKEPTIC One who instinctively or habitually doubts, questions, or disagrees with assertions or generally accepted conclusions.

Skepticism (Also called Pyrrhonism) An ancient Greek school of philosophy taught by Pyrrho of Elis (365?–275 B.C.). Pyrrho studied in India and Persia and taught skepticism at his school in Elis.

SOCRATIC IRONY Pretense of ignorance in a discussion to expose the fallacies in the opponent's logic.

Socrates (470?–399 B.C.) An Athenian teacher and philosopher who advocated this type of discussion, and also the Socratic Method of inquiry and instruction, consisting of a series of questionings, the object of which is to elicit a clear and consistent expression of something supposed to be implicitly known by all rational beings. He was attacked for his contempt for conventional ideas and ways of life and, accused of impiety and of corrupting youth. Socrates defended himself in a speech, intentionally angering instead of soothing the judges. He was condemned to death and drank poison hemlock in prison with his disciples grouped around him (399 B.C.).

SODOMY Any sexual intercourse held to be abnormal, as bestiality; specifically, anal intercourse between two male persons.

Sodom In the Bible, a city destroyed by fire together with a neighboring city, Gomorrah, because of the sinfulness of the people.

SOLECISM A nonstandard usage or grammatical construction; a violation of etiquette; any mistake, impropriety, incongruity.

Soloi, Greece Greek colony which was far removed from the center of Greek civility—Athens. The colonists there spoke a dialect of their own which was much criticized and looked down upon by the Athenians. So *soloikismos*, from which our word *solecism* is derived, meant "speaking incorrectly."

SOLOMON A wise man; sage.

Solomon In the Bible, the king of Israel; son and successor of David, he built the First Temple and was noted for his wisdom.

SOLON A lawmaker or legislator.

Solon (circa 640–559? B.C.) Athenian statesman and lawgiver; he framed the democratic laws of Athens and his name forever after has been a synonym for a lawmaker—especially a wise one.

SOMNOLENT   Sleepy, drowsy.

Somnus   In Roman mythology, the god of sleep. Also evident in such words as: somnambulism, the act or practice of sleepwalking; somniferous, inducing sleep; somniloquy, the habit of talking while asleep; and insomnia, *not* being able to sleep.

SOUSAPHONE   A brass wind instrument of the tuba class; it was devised from the helicon and is used especially in military bands.

John Philip Sousa (1854–1932)   Known as "the March King," he was bandmaster of the U.S. Marine Band from 1880–1892. He then organized his own band and toured the United States and foreign countries with great success. Notable among his many marches are *Semper Fidelis, Liberty Bell, Stars and Stripes Forever,* and *Hands Across the Sea.* The sousaphone was named for him.

SPANIEL   Any of several breeds of dogs characterized by a silky coat, large drooping ears, a small tail, and short legs.

España (Spain)   Over the years "España" became corrupted to "spaniel" and this is what these dogs were called, since they originated in Spain.

SPARTAN   Warlike, brave, hardy, stoical, severe, frugal, highly disciplined.

Sparta One of the two most powerful city-states in ancient Greece. (Athens was the other.) The Spartans lived by extreme self-discipline. At the age of seven, boys began military training and girls, as well, had to pass rigorous tests of physical strength and endurance. Sparta fought a 27-year war with Athens and finally conquered that city. Sparta ruled Athens for about 30 years, but in turn lost it to the Romans, along with the rest of Greece.

SPENCER JACKET A short jacket of an early 19th-century style.

2nd Earl of Spencer, George John Althorp (1758–1834) First Lord of the Admiralty (1794–1801); he showed organizational skill and supervised putting down of several mutinies. He singled out Nelson to command in the Mediterranean, was home secretary (1806–1807), and generally wore the jacket which was forever after to bear his name.

SPENCERIAN Of or characteristic of a style of penmanship taught by Platt Rodgers Spencer.

Platt Rodgers Spencer (1800–1864) An American calligrapher, originator of the Spencerian style of handwriting, teacher of penmanship in schools and business colleges, and author of copybooks and textbooks on penmanship. The Spencerian style is characterized by rounded, well-formed letters.

SPENCERIAN SCIENTIFIC METHOD Of or having to do with the philosophy which attempts to systemize all the sciences into a coherent whole.

Herbert Spencer (1820–1903) An English philosopher, friend of Huxley, Tyndall, George Eliot, and John Stuart Mill, who advocated extreme individualism. He was one of the few thinkers to attempt a systematic account of all cosmic phenomena, including mental and social principles. He influenced contemporary philosophy, psychology, and ethics throughout Europe and America, India, and Japan. He is the author of many books on the subject and is best remembered for his attempt to systemize the sciences.

SPODE A porcelain or chinaware of fine quality.

Josiah Spode (1754–1827) An English potter of Stoke in Staffordshire who made porcelain with paste made of bones (hence bone china) as well as feldspar. He also improved the old blue willow pattern.

SPOONERISM An unintentional transposition of sounds in spoken language.

William Spooner (1844–1930) Much beloved Anglican clergyman and educator, and warden of New College, Oxford, with a tendency to transpose sounds: "blushing crow" for a "crushing blow"; "Let me sew you to your sheet" for "Let me show you to your seat," and so forth.

STANHOPE　A light, open, horse-drawn carriage with two or four wheels and usually one seat.

　Fitzroy Stanhope (1787–1864)　English clergyman for whom the first carriage of this type was built.

STAPELID　Any of a genus of cactus-like African plants of the milkweed family.

　Jan Bode van Stapel (d. 1636)　Dutch botanist.

STENTORIAN　Very loud.

　Stentor　In Greek mythology, a Greek herald in the Trojan war, described in the *Iliad* as having the voice of fifty men.

STETSON　A man's hat worn especially by Western cowboys, usually of felt with a broad brim and a high soft crown.

　John B. Stetson (1830–1906)　Hat maker who trained at his family's hat manufacturing company in Orange, New Jersey, as a boy. He opened his own factory in Philadelphia in 1865. His hats became so popular that working cowboys called all ten-gallon hats "Stetsons" whether they were or not.

STOIC　A person seemingly indifferent to or unaffected by joy, grief, pleasure, or pain.

STOICAL   Indifferent to or unaffected by pleasure or pain, enduring, brave.

The Stoics   A Greek school of philosophy founded by Zeno about 308 B.C., which held that men should be free from passion and calmly accept all occurrences as the unavoidable result of divine will.

STONEWALL   To refuse to budge; to be obdurate in the face of questioning.

Thomas Jonathan "Stonewall" Jackson (1824–1863)   A great American general who fought for the South in the Civil War. He is called "Stonewall" because at the Battle of Bull Run, the first important battle of the Civil War, he and the brigade he commanded "stood like a stone wall," according to the Confederate General Hamilton Bee.

STRADIVARIUS   A famous and much-prized, valuable violin made by A. Stradivari or his sons.

Antonio Stradivari (1644–1737)   Italian violin maker.

STROGANOFF   Cooked with onions, mushrooms and seasonings, with a thick sour-cream sauce.

Count Sergei Grigorievich Stroganoff (1794–1881) Russian official and gourmet. He financed archaeological researches on the shore of the Black Sea, founded and endowed a school of design, served as curator of the Moscow educational district, and ate a lot of the sauce named for him.

STURM UND DRANG   Storm and stress.

Wirrwarr, oder Sturm und Drang   Literally, "confusion, or storm and stress," a play by F. M. v. Klinger (1752–1831), a German dramatist who was a childhood friend of Goethe. He was an officer in the Russian army at St. Petersburg in 1870 and became a lieutenant general in 1811. He is also the author of many other dramatic works and philosophical and realistic novels.

STYGIAN   Dark or gloomy, infernal or hellish.

Styx   In Greek mythology, the river encircling Hades over which Charon ferried the souls of the dead.

SVENGALI   A person who mesmerizes another in order to do his bidding.

Svengali   A character in George du Maurier's 1894 novel *Trilby*. Trilby becomes a famous singer under the influence of Svengali, who was able to hypnotize her into singing beautifully. When Svengali died, so did her career, and soon thereafter so did she.

SYLVAN Of or characteristic of woods or forest regions. **SYLVA** The trees or forest of a region.

Silvanus A Roman god of forest, fields and fertility.

SYLVITE A digestive salt to aid absorption of food.

Franze de la Boe Sylvius (1614–1672) A Prussian-born physician and anatomist, and a professor at Leiden in the west Netherlands. He was a leader in iatrochemistry (medical chemistry) and the first to indicate significance to nodules in lungs in pulmonary tuberculosis.

SYPHILIS A chronic infectious venereal disease. (See VENEREAL.)

Syphilus The hero of a poem by Girolamo Fracastoro (1483–1553) a physician, astronomer, and poet of Verona. The hero, a shepherd, is supposed to have been the first victim of this disease. The poem was published in 1530.

T

TABASCO A trade name for a pungent sauce made from peppers.

Tabasco A state of Mexico in the southeast where the sauce originated.

TACITURN Almost always silent.

Cornelius Tacitus (A.D. 55?–117) A Roman historian whose chief work is a history of the reigns of six Roman emperors. He also wrote a history of the Julian emperors from the death of Augustus. Like most writers, Tacitus preferred to express himself on paper rather than orally.

TAM O' SHANTER A tight-fitting Scottish cap or braided bonnet, sometimes having a pompon, tassel, or feather in the center. Popularly called "tam."

Tam O'Shanter The hero of Robert Burns' poem "Tam O'Shanter," written in 1789.

TANTALIZE To tease or disappoint by promising something desirable and then withholding it.

Tantalus In Greek mythology, a son of Zeus. He was doomed in the lower world to stand in water that always receded when he tried to drink it and under branches of fruit he could never reach.

TARZAN Any very strong, virile, and agile man.

Tarzan The jungle-raised hero of many books by Edgar Rice Burroughs.

TASMANIAN DEVIL A fierce, flesh-eating marsupial.

Abel Janszoon Tasman (1603–1659) Dutch navigator who was sent by Van Diemen, governor general of the Dutch East Indies, on an exploring expedition to Australian waters in 1642. He discovered Tasmania (which he named Van Diemen's land—Van Diemen demurred) and New Zealand. Along the way he met a lot of Tasmanian devils.

TATTERSALL Checkered pattern of dark lines on a light background.

Richard Tattersall (1724–1795) Head of a London horse market and gambler's rendezvous in 1766. He devised the checkered pattern which he used on blankets to distinguish his horses from others.

TAY-SACHS DISEASE A hereditary condition found chiefly among descendants of some Eastern European Jews, caused by an enzyme deficiency and characterized by mental retardation, paralysis, and death in early childhood.

W. Tay (1843–1927) and B. Sachs (1858–1944) An English physician and U.S. neurologist who recognized and described it.

TERPSICHOREAN Having to do with dancing.

Terpsichore In Greek mythology, the Muse of dancing.

TESLA The international unit of magnetic flux density.

Nikola Tesla (1856–1943) U.S. inventor born in Croatia. His other inventions include a system of arc lighting, the Tesla motor and a system of alternating-current transmission, generators of high-frequency currents, a transformer, and wireless systems of communication and power transmission.

THANATOPSIS A view of or musing about death.

Thanatos In Greek mythology, death personified. (Also *thanatology*, the study of death; *thanatophobia*, abnormal fear of death; and *thanato*, dark, cloudy.)

THEREMIN An electronic console-like musical instrument often used for high tremolo effects.

Leo Theremin (1896) A Russian engineer; he invented many electronic instruments which he described as producing "ether-like" music.

THESPIAN An actor or actress.

Thespis Sixth-century Greek poet traditionally considered to be the originator of Greek tragedy.

Those who appeared in his tragedies were called thespians and have been ever since, and even those who appear in comedies may be referred to as thespians, although Thespis didn't write any of *those*.

THUG A rough, brutal hoodlum, gangster, robber, etc.

Thuggee Murder and robbery as once practiced by the thugs of India. The thugs were a religious organization in the service of Kali, a goddess of destruction; their technique was strangulation.

THURSDAY The fifth day of the week.

Thor In Norse mythology, the god of thunder.

TIFFANY SETTING (or mounting) A raised setting in a ring with a jewel held in place by prongs.

Charles L. Tiffany (1812–1902) U.S. jeweler who changed the way rings were set and gave his name to the simplified mounting described above.

TIKI A representative of an ancestor, often a small, sculptured figure worn as an amulet.

Tiki In Polynesian mythology, the first man or the god who created him.

TIMOTHY A type of grass.

Timothy Hanson The gardener who cultivated the grass that bears his name after having brought it from Britain early in the eighteenth century. He was active in cultivating Timothy grass in New York and the Carolinas.

TITIAN A color: reddish-yellow, auburn.

Vecelli or Vecellio Titian (1477–1576) Italian painter who was a protege of Alfonso D'Este, Duke of Ferrara, and Emperor Charles V, two very wealthy and important patrons indeed! Among his works are frescoes, portraits, and religious and mythological pictures. He is known for his intense, rich colors, particularly his reds and yellows.

TOM AND JERRY A hot drink made of alcoholic liquor, beaten eggs, sugar, water or milk, and nutmeg.

Tom and Jerry Characters in sportswriter Pierce Egan's book *Life in London*, published in 1821.

TOMMY GUN A submachine gun.

John Taraferro Thompson (1860–1950) An army officer and inventor of firearms and airplane devices. With Commander John N. Blish, U.S. Navy, he invented the Thompson submachine gun, popularly called the "tommy gun," which was used by Jimmy Cagney, Humphey Bogart, and others in 1930s Warner Bros. movies.

TONY AWARDS   Annual theatrical awards given by New York's American Theater Wing.

Antoinette "Tony" Perry (1888–1949)   An actress, director, and producer who served in several executive capacities on the Theater Wing's board. When she died, they determined to find a way to remember her. In 1949 the United Scenic Artists conducted a contest for a suitable design for an award to be called the "Tony." Herman Rosse's entry, depicting the masks of comedy and tragedy on one side, and the profile of Antoinette Perry on the other, was selected. It continues to be the official Tony award to this day.

TORR   A unit of pressure.

Evangelista Torricelli (1608–1647)   Secretary to Galileo, who had become blind in 1641. After Galileo's death, he succeeded him as the mathematician to the grand duke of Tuscany and professor at Florentine Academy. Also a physicist, he made improvements on the telescope, discovered the principle of the barometer, and devised the earliest form of the instrument in 1643. He also constructed a simple microscope and worked on the cycloid.

TRITON   Any of various chiefly tropical marine mollusks having a pointed, spirally twisted, often colorfully marked shell.

Triton In Greek mythology, a god of the sea, portrayed as having the head and trunk of a man and the tail of a fish. His trumpet is a shell, hence the name of the mollusks.

TUESDAY The third day of the week.
Tiu In Germanic mythology, the god of war and the sky.

TURKEY A large North American bird.
Turkey Country in Asia Minor after which the bird is named. Our North American bird is named after the country Turkey because the name was originally applied to the guinea fowl (with which the American bird was mistakenly identified) first imported by the Portuguese from Africa by way of Turkey.

TUXEDO A man's tailless, semi-formal jacket for evening wear, originally black and with satin lapels; a dinner jacket.
Tuxedo Country Club A club at Tuxedo Park near Tuxedo Lake, New York, where tuxedos were first popularized when Griswold Lorillard introduced them circa 1886. He had brought the style back from England.

TYPHOID MARY A carrier of a disease, typhoid especially, but designating any disease carrier.

"Typhoid" Mary Mallon   A cook in New York (d. 1938). She did not have typhoid herself and never got it, but she was a carrier, and gave the disease to many people. Her name is now a synonym for a carrier of any disease.

U

UTOPIA   Any idealized place, state, or situation of perfection.

Utopia   An imaginary island described in a book of the same name by Sir Thomas More (1516) as having a perfect political and social system. In Greek, *utopia* means "no place."

V

VALERIAN   Any of the genus of the plants of the valerian family; also a drug made from the roots of the garden heliotrope, formerly used as a sedative and antispasmodic.

Valerian (A.D. *190?–260*)   Roman emperor from 253–260. He tried to stop the Persian conquest of

Syria and Armenia. At first he was successful but was finally overpowered and defeated by Shapur I at Edessa (260). He was held in captivity until his death.

VAN DYKE   A short, pointed beard.

Sir Anthony Van Dyck (1599–1641) Flemish painter who studied under Rubens and was his assistant on some of his great canvases. He was knighted by Charles I of England in 1632 and appointed court painter. He is best known in artistic circles for his portraits of Charles I and members of the English royal family and English notables of the period, but he is known in *all* circles as the originator of the short, neat, pointed beard he habitually wore—the van dyke.

VANITY FAIR   Any place, society, etc., regarded as dominated by folly, frivolity, and show.

Vanity Fair   In Bunyan's *Pilgrim's Progress*, a fair, always going on in the town of Vanity, symbolic of worldly folly, frivolity, and show.

VEAL OSCAR   A rich entree of veal, crab meat, asparagus, and hollandaise sauce.

Oscar Tschirky (1856–1950) Legendary Swiss chef, known as "Oscar of the Waldorf," originally with the Hoffman House and Delmonico's in New

York City and identified with the Waldorf-Astoria Hotel from its opening in 1893. He created the Veal Oscar and many other dishes.

VENEREAL Of or pertaining to sexual intercourse.

Venus The Roman goddess of love and beauty, identified with the Greek goddess Aphrodite. (See APHRODISIAC.)

VENN DIAGRAMS Diagrams which illustrate symbolic logic.

John Venn (*1834–1923*) English logician and man of letters; he was a teacher of logic and author of *The Logic of Chance* (1866), *Symbolic Logic* (1881), and *The Principles of Empirical Logic* (1889).

VICTORIA A low, light, four-wheeled carriage.

Queen Victoria (*1819–1901*) Queen of the United Kingdom of Great Britain and Ireland and from 1876, empress of India. Her carriage was low-hung to allow her to enter without having to climb steps. By 1851 when her popularity was at its peak this type of low-hung phaeton was already being referred to as a "victoria." It was her favorite conveyance.

VOLCANO A vent in the earth's surface through which molten rock, rock fragments, gases, etc. are ejected.

VULCANIZE The process of treating rubber in order to increase its strength.

Vulcan Roman god of fire and metalworking.

W

WAHHABI Any member of a strict Moslem sect which adheres closely to the Koran.

Abdul Wahhab (1703–1792?) Founder of the sect which still flourishes in Saudi Arabia.

WALDORF SALAD A salad made chiefly of apples, celery, nuts, and mayonnaise.

The Waldorf-Astoria Hotel Hotel in New York City, built in 1893. The salad was no doubt invented by its creative chef, Oscar. (See VEAL OSCAR.)

WANKEL ENGINE A rotary combustion engine having a spinning piston and requiring fewer parts and much less fuel than used in a comparable turbine engine.

Felix Wankel (1902) German engineer and inventor who conceived the Wankel engine.

WASSERMANN TEST A diagnostic test for syphilis. (See SYPHILIS.)

August Von Wassermann (1866–1925) A German bacteriologist; he discovered this test for syphilis in 1906.

WATT A unit of electrical power. Also wattage, the amount of electrical power expressed in watts, and the watt hour, a unit of electrical energy or work, with one watt representing one hour of work.

James Watt (1736–1819) A Scottish mechanical engineer, inventor, and mathematical-instrument maker. He made many improvements on the steam engine. He held the patents for many inventions, including an ink for copying manuscripts (patented 1780) and an apparatus for reproducing sculpture. Watt was the first to use the term *horsepower*. The watt, a unit of power, is named in his honor.

WAVELLITE A phosphate of aluminum, vitreous and translucent.

Archibald Percival Wavell, 1st Earl Wavell (1883–1950) Discoverer of the phosphate which is named after him. He was educated at the Royal Military College at Sandhurst in preparation for a career in service. He served in the Boer War, on the Indian frontier, and in World Wars I and II. He was commander-in-chief of the British forces in India in 1941, and the next year supreme commander in the southwest Pacific. In 1943 he was in charge of Allied forces in India and Burma. From 1943–1947 he served as viceroy of India. In between battles, he had time to discover the phosphate which bears his name.

WEDGWOOD   A type of pottery or china, typically with classical figures in white cameo relief on an unglazed blue or black background.

Josiah Wedgwood (1730–1795)   English potter who modeled his designs after the remains of Pompeii and Greek vases. His oldest daughter was the mother of Charles Darwin.

WEDNESDAY   The fourth day of the week.

Woden   The chief Teutonic god, often identified with the Norse god Odin.

WELLINGTON BOOT   A high boot, traditionally extending just above the knee in front and just below in back, now usually just below the knee.

1st Duke of Wellington, Arthur Wellesley (1769–1852)   British statesman and general, popularly called the "Iron Duke," was prime minister of England from 1828–1830 and much admired for the boots he wore, which came to be called by his name.

WELSBACH BURNER   A trademark for a gas burner with a gauze mantel impregnated with thorium oxide and cerium oxide; when lighted the gauze gives off an incandescent, greenish light.

C. A. Welsbach (1858–1929) Austrian chemist who was also a baron; his invention did a great deal to make life during the gaslight era brighter.

WHEATSTONE BRIDGE A divider circuit used for the measure of electrical resistance; a device containing such a circuit.

Sir Charles Wheatstone (1802–1875) An English physicist and inventor who carried on researches in electricity, light, and sound. He suggested the stereoscope, demonstrated velocity of electricity in a conductor, and devised an electric telegraph for transmitting messages, which was patented in 1837. As though that wasn't enough, he also made improvements on the dynamo, invented the concertina in 1837, an automatic telegraph, the kaleidosophon, and the device for which's he's best remembered—the circuit called the Wheatstone bridge.

WIENIE or WIENER A type of smoked sausage similar to a frankfurter. (See FRANKFURTER.)

Wienerwurst Literally, *Vienna sausage,* since *Wien* is German for Vienna, where it was first made.

WINCHESTER RIFLE A breechloading repeating rifle.

Oliver Winchester (1810–1880) Industrialist who bought control of an arms-manufacturing company in New Haven, Connecticut. He acquired repeating-rifle inventions of various inventors and manufactured them, very successfully.

WISTERIA   Any of several climbing wood vines of the genus *Wisteria*.

Caspar Wistar (1761–1818)   A Philadelphia professor of anatomy and author of *System of Anatomy* (1811), the first American textbook on this subject. He wasn't a botanist, nor did he discover the beautiful wisteria vine on some exotic travels. However, he had good friends, including Thomas Nuttall, who named the wisteria plant after him.

WOLLASTONITE   A mineral, a native calcium silicate.

William H. Wollaston (1766–1828)   English physicist who discovered palladium in 1804 and rhodium in 1805. He devised a method of making platinum malleable. In optics, he invented reflecting lenses, a camera lucia (an optical device that projects an image onto a plane surface, especially for tracing), and Wollaston's doublet, a form of magnifying glass for converting spherical aberrations. But he's best remembered in mineralogy classes for discovering the calcium silicate named for him.

WORCESTERSHIRE SAUCE   A piquant sauce of soy, vinegar, and spices.

Worcester, England   A county in west central England where the sauce originated.

WORSTED   A smooth, hard-twisted thread or yarn made from long wool; fabric made from this, with a smooth, hard surface.

Worsted (now Worstead), England   Place where the first worsted was made.

WULFENITE   Yellow lead ore.

Franz X. von Wulfen (1728–1805)   An Austrian mineralogist and discoverer of the ore.

X

XANADU   A place of idyllic beauty.

Xanadu   An imaginary locality in Samuel Taylor Coleridge's poem "Kubla Khan," which begins "In Xanadu did Kubla Khan/A stately pleasure dome decree/Where Alph, the sacred river ran/Through caverns measureless to man/Down to a sunless sea."

XANTHIPPE   An ill-tempered woman.

Xanthippe (5th century B.C.) Wife of Socrates; she was the prototype of the quarrelsome, nagging wife. (See SOCRATIC IRONY.)

Y

YAGI A VHF or UHF directional antenna widely used for TV reception in weak signal areas.

Hidetsugu Yagi 20th-century Japanese engineer who invented it.

YARBOROUGH A bridge or whist hand containing no card higher than a nine.

Charles Anderson Worsely, Earl of Yarborough Famous sportsman of the late Victorian era; he reportedly offered a standing bet of 1,000 to 1 against its turning up in any game he played in (and he played in many). According to statisticians the odds of this happening are actually 1,827 to 1 against the appearance of a yarborough.

YOUNGBERRY A large, sweet, dark-purple berry, a cross between a blackberry and a dewberry.

B. M. Young 19th-century U.S. horticulturist and berry fancier who kept planting blackberries and dewberries in opposite rows until he got the offspring he'd worked for—a new kind of berry which he promptly christened the youngberry, and which is very hard to find in markets anywhere.

Z

ZEALOT A fanatically committed person.

Zealots Members of a Jewish sect who committed mass suicide rather than be captured as slaves. At the fortress of Masada in A.D. 73 some 960 Zealots faced the 6,000-man Tenth Roman Legion. Hopelessly outnumbered, they chose to die as free men rather than be captured.

ZEEMAN EFFECT The effect produced upon the structure of the spectrum lines of light emitted or absorbed by atoms subject to a moderately strong magnetic field, resulting in the splitting of each spectrum line into two or three lines.

Pieter Zeeman (1865–1943) Dutch physicist who discovered (with H. A. Lorentz) the phenomenon known as the Zeeman effect, and with Lorentz was awarded the 1902 Nobel prize for physics as a result.

ZEPPELIN A rigid airship having a long, cylindrical body supported by internal gas cells.

Ferdinand von Zeppelin (1838–1917) German soldier and airship designer; he constructed the first airship which was to bear his name in 1900. Unfortunately it was wrecked in landing. Nevertheless he persisted and constructed a factory in Germany (Friedrichshafen) for the construction of airships of rigid types known as zeppelins and was active in building them for many years. (See HINDENBURG.)

ZINNIA Any of a genus of plants (*Zinnia*) of the composite family, having colorful flower heads, native to North and South America.

J. G. Zinn (d. 1759) A German physician and botanist, author of the first book on the anatomy of the eye. Linnaeus, the famous Swedish botanist and father of modern systematic botany, was a friend of Zinn's and, needing a new name for a new species, Linnaeus thoughtfully named the Zinnia after his learned friend.

ZOROASTRIANISM The religious system set forth in the Zend-Avesta, teaching the worship of Ormazd in the context of a universal struggle between the forces of light and darkness.

Zoroaster Persian prophet of the 6th-century, founder of Zoroastrianism.

Pocket-Size Writing Guides from Webster's New World™

Vinyl-jacketed, palm-sized guides that are ideal quick reference guides for school, home, or office

Webster's New World™ Pocket Dictionary
David B. Guralnik, Editor in Chief

Based upon *Webster's New World Dictionary, College Edition*, this best-selling compact includes appendices on American presidents. common abbreviations, weights and measures, nations of the world, and much more! 0-671-41826-2/$3.95

Webster's New World™ Dictionary of Acronyms and Abbreviations
Auriel Douglas and Michael Strumpf

More than15,000 common and not-so-common acronyms and abbreviations drawn from a variety of fields—business, government, computer terminology, academia, sports, and many others—all fully defined. 0-13-947136-7/$7.95

Webster's New World™ Guide to Punctuation

A handy reference tool to the rules of correct usage for any form of punctuation from the period to the asterisk to quotation marks. Includes a glossary on the parts of speech and a concise history of each punctuation mark.
0-13-947896-5/$5.95

Webster's New World™ Guide to Spelling
Auriel Douglas and Michael Strumpf

An easy-to-use guide to the fundamental techniques and simple rules (and exceptions to those rules) of English spelling.
0-13-948043-9/$5.95

Webster's New World™ Speller/Divider
Compiled by Shirley M. Miller

Based on *Webster's New World™ Dictionary of the American Language, Second College Edition*, this book is a quick, accurate, up-to-date guide to correct spelling and syllabification of more than 33,000 words.
0-671-44183-6/$4.95

Build Your Library Of Webster's New World™ Compact Guides At Your Local Bookstore!